Half of the Battle is to Surrender All I Have

(Poetry Songbook)

Created & Written by Adrienna "Deo" Turner

authorHOUSE

AuthorHouse™
1663 Liberty Drive
Bloomington, IN 47403
www.authorhouse.com
Phone: 833-262-8899

Published by AuthorHouse 08/25/2020

ISBN: 978-1-4343-9306-7 (sc)
ISBN: 978-1-4670-3212-4 (e)

Print information available on the last page.

This book is printed on acid-free paper.

Dedications

To all my friends and family members for all the encouragement, love and support whom were there from the beginning to the end of this journey. There is a battle we all have to face, struggles we have to overcome, and pain we have to gain strength from! These rhymes, songs, and poems are secular. It is a doorway to open up to a mere image of me, you, and us. Turn our lives over to Jesus!

Table of Contents

Love, Romance, Relationships, Compassion Poem Selection

Historical, Real Life Stories Poem Selection

Comedic Poem Selection

Miscellaneous & Hardcore Poems Section

Love, Romance, Relationships, Compassion Poem Selection

More than Love © 7/12/2002

Everyday I'm with you, feels like a dream
Pinch me
Wake me up
More than what it seems
Add the strawberry and the whip cream
So good
Doing all I could
To satisfy
I will testify
You make me feel like I can fly
So high
So high
Off your love, brings tears of joy
Glad you're my boy
A caramel delight
Making love all night
'Til the daylight
Satisfying my appetite

This feeling
Got me crawling to the ceiling
In need of sexual healing
So appealing
This is more than love
More than anything I've ever felt before
When you walked through that door

What's your mission?
Wishing
To make love, kissing
Please listen
To my body calling
Stalling
Falling
Deeper in love
Higher than smoking on a dub
Rubbing me down in the bathtub
Bubble bath
Strawberries fed to me, making me laugh

This feeling
Got me crawling to the ceiling
In need of sexual healing
So appealing
This is more than love
More than anything I've ever felt before
When you walked through that door

Find the Depths of My Soul © 11/12/2002

Find the depths of my soul
Explore, endure, and take full control
Came to me like the wind
Invisible glare
Are you standing there?
Give me a sign
Goal driven
With you involved in my life, keeps me livin'
As I watch you in action
A beautiful smile gives me pure satisfaction
Laying here next to you
Thinking about what I can do
To show you that this love I am feeling is true
No more playing, no more phone numbers
No more carrying rubbers
For secret encounters to satisfy this heat
You tamed it
You are all I want: from the top of your head down to your feet
Thrown all the negative baggage away
Only think about you--day by day

God sends me the one that I can share
Oh you express how much you care
Not just a one-night affair
Someone that will always be there
Find the depths of my soul
Lady, you are the only one that I have searched for
Well, you have found me
Encouraged me at times when I did not love myself
Show me grow with me
Doing everything and anything in my power to make you happy

The head of my household
Take care of the finances and arguments when they unfold
Hold me closer and closer to your side
Hold my hand
Let me know that I am the man
I will take care of this situation
God made such a beautiful creation
The angel in my life that I dream of
Entangled, entwined in love
Search my deepest fantasies
One look in your eyes is a taste of ecstasy

Try to hide these emotions
What's your secret potion?
You got me wrapped, sprung
Falling deeper and deeper until I'm hung
You got me forever
To leave you, never
I cannot imagine being separated
No argument should escalate
Forgive me, live with me
Love me continue to hold me

God sends me one that I can share
Oh you expressed how much you care
Not just a one-night affair
Someone that will always be there
Find the depths of my soul
Lady, you are the only one that searched for
You found me, when I could not find myself
Show me grow with me
Doing everything and anything in my power to make you happy

Touch my Bad Side © 8/1993

Attack
See so many tracks
Shooting up on crack
One less man around
Roll up a towel over your gun to make no sound
Everyone got a bad side
Tales from the dark side
Turn the other cheek
Fools pulling up at the creek
Gun pointed: no time to think
Gun fired
The second you blink
Not uptight
Just treat me right
In the morning, found dead
Room shattered with all red
Scattered
Down a ladder, to some, it did not matter
Listening to chit-chatter
Check witnesses to see if they've seen anything
Nothing but a one-night fling
Don't get mad
'Cause I was the best lover you ever had
Learn to love
Just a memory: left thinking of
Don't judge a book by its cover
Could unleash a woman like no other

❄

This poem deals with a one-night stand that leads to a silent death.

❄

Hard to Love Thee © 5/20/2005

Hard to love thee
Seriously
To be so lovely
Sorry
But you will not play me like Atari
If you don't know what you are dealing with
Move real swift
Not knowing what hit
Can supply pure pleasure
That no one can measure
Worth a treasure!
Not a sex symbol
Or a limbo
Ready to stroll
Because this sister is on a roll
Low-down bums trying to score
This female is hardcore
No goodie-good shoes
Got your girl singing the blues
Because she sees you with me
Nothing ever happened
If your girl only knew how you can truly be
Premeditated murder, killing him with a knife
Was it self-defense, serving life?
The judicial system and jury had no sympathy for a battered wife
In for death row
A woman that was once mellow
Until he caused me to let go with one blow

This poem is refers to a promiscuous relationship and how a battered wife killed the man she once loved.

Sex on the Brain © 10/2/2005

I was messing around with a true blue
Had no clue
If I had only knew
What would happen to you?
We first met outside a project complex
Blind date, not meant for me
Sex
Happened next
First time, I felt such strength
Sexing me to a 7-hour length
Power drill
A brother that gave me chills, for real
He filled my sexual appetite
Night after night
Cousin drove from Moreno Valley to Riverside
Then to San Bernardino, as you jumped in the ride
We talked, we walked
Made out at the park until the dogs barked
Opened me up, brought the freaky side out
But it was not what I was all about
Girl trapped in fleshly lusts
Christ to enter in this vessel was a must
God is who I trust
I had to let this go
Moved back to Milwaukee with my mother, even though
I could not let you go
Sexual appetite was beyond me
Missed you intimately
As I looked at our relationship, nothing else you could offer
You wanted 10 kids out of wedlock, only loving you under covers
You made plans to live with your mother
I wanted more like an education: college
Something you could not acknowledge
Wanting to go deeper, how deep was your love?
Looking at your plans and what you were really made of
Unable to leave the club
Smoking on a dub
Could not escape the moment of rape
Whose the blame for giving up the butt
Called me a slut
But, you did not know my story until it flowed from my lips
Only believed what was said on the streets, get a grip
Until you saw the herpes around his lips

Ain't that a trip
I needed some fresh air instead of standing there
You gave me this sexual stare
As I walked in the bathroom to fix my hair
Ended the relationship with one more night of sexual pleasure
The fact that I left you in the dark room after a long lecture
To leave you, painted a broken picture
Thought our relationship was secure
After this one night of sexual pleasure

Back in the Daze © 2/1994

People keep bugging
Wanting something
Hustling and mugging
While we all are struggling
Life isn't easy
Having 8 kids at 25, is that sleazy?
Just looking for someone to please me
Met men in the Army, Navy
Eating beans, rice and gravy
Oh God save me
From this hellhole, 9th new-born baby
Seems like mother's go through frustrations to nurture
Paying my son's bail
Without a father in home, unable to raise them well
As my new lover says, "Farewell"
Don't need your advice, can't you tell
Is there a Mr. Right?
After meeting you tonight
One-night stand, end up in a fight
After fulfilling our sexual appetite
Its no secret
I am not into religion or God's Word, don't want to hear it
Get it
Saving coins in a cookie jar
Showing skin in the local bar
No real goals or ambitions, praying for my superstar
Tired of your judging me, criticism
Not kidding 'em
Racism
Don't make me laugh, change 360 degrees
Back where I started, freeze
Ended up in the slammer
Ramming my head in the stone walls like a hammer
Another female turned this mutha out
Sitting in my bed, in doubt
What was my life truly all about?

When writing this poem, this is a dedication to all the single mothers that are searching for love and do not want to be alone. However, this poem had a twist! This female ended up looking for love in the wrong places and ended up in jail due to making the wrong choices in her life.

How could you snap? © 10/5/2005

I feel your presence, watching how you eye-balled me
You got me feeling so sexy
Stepped into your Lex-us
Took me to the motel for sex, screaming out Je-sus
I was wrong to scream out another man's name
Also putting God's name in vain
Down with your tricks and sex game
Another woman walked through the door, with no name
Dang
I snapped
Knuckles cracked
Female got jacked
Unpacked
Fool had no jimmy hats
I grabbed my clothes and noticed the owner
Outside smoking a cigarette around the corner
It was around 11 o'clock
Loud sounds filled the air around the block
In the motel room I exit, he did not stop
As the bed knocks
Kicking off his socks
I opened the door, he acted like a wild fox
As if Hercules was trapped in a box
For so long
Going at that cat, strong
The owner finally made a call
A body in the other room was ripped raw
Body parts and blood all over the wall
A female that made the wrong choice by meeting some psycho
at the dance hall
Glad I was not her
This night was a blur

Dance floor © 10/5/2005

People surrounded the dance floor, dancing
Men sweating me, glancing
A man stepped in the club; he must have some loot
I can tell, just look at his Armani suit
He stepped up to me, telling me that I was cute
Oh shoot!
Started blushing
Emotions flushing
Adrenaline rushing
To tell my girls, as they cheered me on
Walked back on the dance floor, dancing to my song
Thinking this honey, sure needs some money
Sister is not trying to be funny
Bills need to be paid
With his money flow, I could hire a maid
Spin me around in your escapade
I am not afraid
To share my feelings, what's on my mind
As your hands glide down my side to my behind
Interpersonal or my perception
We will need protection
Digging in my purse, looking for my conceptive
Condoms, I don't have time for any rejection
My girls appear to be jealous
Uptight and rebellious
Hot lotion in my purse, a kiss I blow
Do you feel my flow?
Strawberry flavor
Can make you change your behavior
What you don't know, won't hurt
Kissing me and putting me to work
Are you nervous? Your eyes are blinking
What are you thinking?
I knew from before
Once you came through that door
Went back to his place, in the bedroom, coat fell to the floor
My loving is what you will adore
Easy to love and hard to leave
Believe, what you want to believe
Let me tell you that my hair is not a weave
You best to believe
Satisfying, perspiring, as if he had a trick up his sleeve
Sista got what she came for, this is what I really need
Caught up in a web of greed

Just another Old Tune © 3/1994

Throw on some Jodeci or whatever you got
To make me sweat and get hot
To put your lover on the spot
Get in the romantic mood, one kiss
Taste of this will leave him lost in the abyss
Boy, you cannot resist
Of sexual desires
Body hot like fire
Pulling things from under your belt
Having feelings you never felt
Body in so much heat
R&B tunes that make you wanna melt
Usher, Teena Marie, Brian McKnight
Under some candlelight
Isley brothers, Teddy Pendergrass, and Marvin Gaye
On a highway to love, let the music play
Sway to the left and sway to the right
Oh this music feels so right
'Between the sheets' is when I think of you
Feels like I have been here before, like de ja vu
'For the Love of You'
For all the things I do
Willing to do 'Anything' like the song by 3T
Come to me baby to pure ecstasy
Weak to your knees
'Keep it Comin', please
Playing Janet Jackson, 'Someday is Tonight'
'Lets wait awhile' to do it just right
'Turn off the lights'
To hold this body tight
'Do me baby' like Bell Biv DeVoe
Watch it grow, grow and grow
Take it slow
Don't rush it too fast, take me away
Like Calgon body wash and spray
'Knockin the boots' with some H-town
To go downtown
El Debarge is a smooth brother with high notes
Guy, Babyface is another, that's all she wrote
'50 candles' and 'Slow Wine'
Songs to unwind
By the fireplace with a man that is so fine
'Just kickin it' with a nucca you figure

14

His body is much bigger
To take his love to my hidden treasures
Taking it to any measure
For his sexual pleasures
Out in the rain
Making love to my membrane
Driving me totally insane
Adrenaline following, feeling the pain
Pounding, twirling and shaking like a hurricane
Playing some Al B Sure to ease the pain
Sade, Yannie, and Kenny G make you want to slip away
On an island with some smooth rhythms from Maxwell to serenade

Look into these slanted eyes © 3/28/2006

Scooping into these slanted eyes
Funny how time flies
As you place your lips on my lips
Watching my butt move side to side
Pheening for what is between these thighs
Bragging you are a pimp
Cannot just pick one
Living my teen years to have fun
Only have one life to live
Receive the love that I have to give
Your wish is my every command
Your needs are on demand
To fulfill and deliver
Knees knocking and body starts to shiver
Love flows deeper than a river
Down to the roots
Only focusing on knocking the boots
Even though the guy is cute
And pockets full of loot
Why don't you just admit the truth
Speaking to a sex therapist similar to Dr. Ruth
Then find you with her in the phone booth
Legs twitchin'
Hormones listenin'
Involves more than kissin'
Wishin'
I never saw what I saw
Enter the pimp-mactress dimension
Of playing him in return
Playing my cards right, watch him burn
His private hot like fire
Messed with a whore that did up the entire empire
I could have gave you what you were missing
Only if you followed your heart and mind
My lips you would still be kissing
Got a bad one when you were fishing
For your sexual appetite
Ouch, what a bite!
All started from one look in your slanted eyes
Getting burned from sex with another came as a surprise...

Web of Love © 2/9/2004

Captured in your web of love
A whisper from God above
That you were heavenly sent
To spend our lives together was meant
Reading God's Holy Word from that day forth
Acknowledging my woman's worth
Jumping to my every need
Following your lead
Removed all the pain and hurt
Turned your head on every woman that flirt
Faithful, not a man trying to cover up the dirt
Later caught you sexing with other women, you pleasured
Your wife—you should have treasured
My love to the fullest
Makin' me lose it
Can't live without your love
Caught up in the web of love
Sprung, wrapped up into you
A man that I thought could be true

Love Unknown © 2002, 1996

You're always on my mind
You're the love that I'm trying to find
If I could fly like a bird
To reach you, the melodies float through my head from every word
I would go to that extent to be heard
If any tears are shed
I'm here to fill good thoughts in your head
My thoughts become your thoughts eventually
My body, my emotions, becomes your mentally
Soar over every mountain
Overflow through every fountain
To feel your love flow through my veins
Absolutely searching for every portion it contains
All that it reveals the presence of you gives me chills
This love I feel for you is essential
Never want to hurt a man with so much potential
Extremely astounding
Leaving my heart pounding
Drowning in your undying passion that I can't resist
Continue to persist
Until our love collides
With the innermost feelings inside
As long as exists

A Murder Date © 4/1997

The public defender
Had a message sender
To give me an invitation to dinner
Very intellectual
Treated me as an individual
Not as a client
Or a sex object
A man who once lived in the projects
Something I would never suspect
Went to his private ranch
Raining and hid under a tree branch
Walked inside, noticed several pad locks
Why did he need so many locks?
Security everywhere, seeing anyone that steps up to his door to knock
Sat down on the couch getting all cozy
Kissing, feeling on me, so lovy-dovy
Asking me, 'Do you love me?'
He would definitely qualify
Yet something about this man, left me terrified
Why?
We had so much fun
Stepped in his bedroom and noticed a machine gun
Looked around, all the doors locked
Watching the hands on the clock
Tick-tock
Asking myself, 'Am I going to die?'
Time passing by
A tear rolled down my eye
He entered the room, saying "Hi"
A nervous feeling aroused and slightly shy
Started to sweat and perspire
He pulled out the electrical wire
Has my life expired
What a fake, liar, and have been deceived
It was time to leave
All the lovely things I received
Had a price to pay, but not worth dying
Trying to scream
Wake me up Lord from this bad dream

Met at a Party © 3/8/2008

Met this man at a party
Introduced me to somebody
This is how it all started
He turned out to be so cold-hearted
A cold-blooded horny reptile
Boasted to his friends how he liked my style
Played and dangled ladies with his versatile
A passion a woman could not hold inside
He was a charmer, lover, and emotions on a tide
Dead silence
He provoked, women he choked with sexual violence
Petrified harder I tried
The more I lied
There was no where I could hide
He was on my path and trailed me down
Run out of the building once I seen his face around
Later he was on America's Most Wanted
Bounty hunters and cops hunted
He was banned from bars as an outlaw
How could a man be so raw
At one time, he forced me to strip
He busted my bottom lip
Had no family members to call
Man lost his sanity
Pictures of him with a gold-tee
Someone please help me

Whispers in the Dark © 4/1997

In the club, spotting a hot male
Thought he was all that, because I could tell
Asked me to come back to his house
Heard him calling his spouse
What did this fool thought?
He would not get caught
No date
Forced himself on me, yelling "rape"
He locked the door and closed the curtain drapes
Tried to take advantage
In so much rage
Left a gun in the trunk
Time to let this fool feel the funk
Aimed at his face for talking so much junk
Later I spoke with psychic friends
Said this man will be giving up his ends
To keep his story quiet, pretend
Act like it never happened, I ain't no hooker
On T.J. Booker
On some other woman, he went down south
Red flaming bumps around his mouth
Kicked him out
Like Lot delivered from Sodom and Gomorrah, 'Don't look back'
Ran as fast as you can before the fire attack
Out in the open hoping
Someone would notice and call the police
To stop this wild beast
He did not care the least
Pulled out mace in his face
This swine only had sex on his mind
Paranoid syndrome
Sexual assault was forced on me in his home
His sexual actions happened to at least eleven
Praying for it to stop to God in heaven
Staggered out of my nightmare
Started to swear
I would destroy him, he got my word
My story will be heard
Terrified since this man was going through his phallic stage
Did not care about my age
I was ready to fight
Out for spite
With a case of knives, this man screamed for his life

Some believe, 'Eye for an Eye'
Can you experience watching a man die?
Psychosexual behavior
Sex with a child is worse than making out with your neighbor
So much abstraction
Buts and pieces of your life becomes just a fraction
In this 'Brave New World'
Reinforce your boys and girls
To observe their social imitation with peers and adults
All the blame and excuses alone is not the parents' fault

Catch me while U can © 7/1997

You act like a Be-Devil
Rebel got to be on my level
On contempt for being a pimp
Naked men in coats
Broke want to ride the boat
Barge whose in charge
When you're living large
Fools selling telling smelling
Like liquor
Blood gets thicker
Heart beats quicker
When death creeps
Thoughts float while I sleep
Your crew was rolling deep
Got high in my bathroom with a stash
Your boys got smashed
Dash as two cars crash
Jump out of the car
Not too far
There was a raid
Of dope-dealers wanting to get paid
Then the car explodes
Money comes in loads
Bodies erode
Paid a good attorney
Afterwards, seeking another journey
Not to be with a man just cuz I'm horny
Another jerk I see
All flirty to work me

Out for One Thang © 7/1997

Kicking it with the 'Get Fresh Crew'
At a house party, looking for someone to screw
The last girl he slept with smelled like mildew
Only made out with her because she said, "I want to do you"
Another top cat
Believes he is all that
And a bag of chips, spicy Doritos
Eating some beef burritos
His stomach was bloated
Taking some Pepto Bismol tablets double coated
So full of bull
Spoke a mouthful
Now you are in debt
Over a bet
And regret the girl you slept with
Blaming the Bacardi
While you were at the party
Too drunk and unable to see anybody
Down to get your groove on
Made a move on
Mercy, Mercy me
Desiring me sexually
Demanding but not so understanding
I want a man I can treasure
Instead of one time sexual pleasure
Met you again on tour
Taking you places that you never explored
Claim you have sex only because you are bored
Mi amor
On the 'Gank move to Skeeze'
Willing to beg on your knees
To get with deez
Low top Cadillac Deville
If looks could kill
You have that appeal
Tightly sealed
Rubbing and looking between my thighs
Checking out your size

Historical, Real Life Stories
Poem Selection

Manifest Destiny © 3/1997

Native Americans manifest destiny
Memory of a stolen land is in the back of their minds for centuries
Europeans tried to rewrite history
Believed that Custer was their hero
Found crushed and sliced to zero
Christopher Columbus supposed to be the first to discover the world
Labeled as a 'founder', just hurled
On a boat, he twirled
In his own mischief to steal the land known
Are we called Americans or Indians?
Incentive to get all he could take
Left the land bare
All their resources and assets taken from under them
With government laws with a signature of an X
Unable to change history from so far back
There were Native Americans hands slashed for gold
Refused to come home with none, his men would unfold
Dead remained in the cold
Movies that explain what happen in the Black Hills
Does it clear the pain one feels?
Blood flowing down
Homeless for months and illness crept in the land
American language was forced to comprehend
Indians once ruled this Continent
Ancient leaders foretold that those will be sent
To suffer migration, immigration, land separated
More than they anticipated
Great struggle and fought great battles
Homeland taken including horses and cattle's
Seven Prophecies forced the splitting of families
Promised to move the large cities with salaries
But only found no jobs, owing your month rent
Little money from government, all spent
Alcohol was the remedy to all non-sense
Plan turned out to be at one's great expense
Indian Appropriation Act stopped all treaty-making
Another method for the government to keep taking
Land as the treaties were broken
Which enabled the property to be open
Five Civilized Tribes resisted
American leaders persisted
To keep their land and insisted
To build schools and towns

Cherokee's build everything with their bare hands from the ground
U.S. feared Native Americans bringing in their 'old traditions'
Trained and taught on reservations
English culture, turn from what they once knew
Burned everything they once had, ashes
Today, we are accepting other cultures and religions
What a switch in time

Sioux Struggle © 3/1997

Black Hills on the market
What a beautiful land of which the U.S. fought to take
Court of Claims heard and rejected twenty four cases
The land was in stake
Ralph Case, a Sioux lawyer made a series of mistakes
There was no confidential evidence
As the years grew more tense
Lazarus and Sonosky took over the expense
Later, these two men were rich
Ten million dollars and owned the Black Hills
Many believe it was confiscated
The Sioux tribes were deviated
Including anyone related
Mixed blood were not accommodated
Only full bloods were compensated
There was no land or no pay
Waiting for decades to get a piece of their land
Will history repeat itself again?
Congressional Act in 1877
Verified it was U.S. government property
One huge monopoly
Able to buy or sell sections of the land until nothing
Sections were divided on the map, so becoming
With a list of Indian offenses
To take control over Indian defenses
Afraid they would rise up as a nation
So they established schools and camps of concentration
Complete humiliation of God's creation
Hair was cut, separated from families, isolation
The Battle of Sugar Point interrogated
Prorated, only demonstrated
Hostility towards Indians, arresting them on any occasion
Did not approve of their ways of praising
Their God and the earth
Formed a jurisdiction for anything to throw their heads in the dirt
Selling their land for not what it was worth
Sioux whole being seeing
Their own beliefs and identity
Destroyed their language, life style, and crushed to entity
Is it all lost for all affinity
Red Cloud and his warriors hid in the trees
To leave Fetterman and his troops on their knees
Killing eighty or so men

Setting foot in a place where they've never been
Thinking Indians would mend
Their differences and take what they wanted
Out numbered as the guns were pointed
Indians will not surrender, kill or be killed
Born as a warrior, already rage instilled
The battle was short and fierce
'Custer Massacre' in the seventh Calvary
And General George Custer body was pierced
Something they never witnessed before
In Indian Territory, annihilated quickly, falling to the floor
Most Indians were known for their bravery
As others were forced into slavery

Indian Movement © 3/1997

In 1887, Indians were forced to accept allotments
Had to move out of their residents
Walking miles in the cold, unsure where they would be sent
Some believe it was a nightmare meant
It was foretold by the old
With visions of the white man being so cold
Evil spirits within
Teaching us about sin
Willing to do anything to feed their families
As their land was sold
Black Hills was noted for gold
The Ute tribe from Colorado was the first
Allotments and other tribes were treated much worse
Many died
From hunger and tried
To survive as the white man lied
The 'Trail of Tears', we all cried
Took our lives and culture
Kids off to boarding schools for torture
Started by an old militant soldier
Died in the desert, hawking with blood-thirsty vultures
Learned skills of hunting, fishing and trapping
Alcohol was introduced by settlers, Indians snapping
Because what they were forced to adapt to
Land sold for cheap
Borrowing against rations to eat
Debt was steep
Many feel into a hole dug too deep
Unable to read and write, hard to understand
Laws created by the white man
The 'Burke Act' opened doors to sell Indian land
'Dawes Act' delays 25 years to sell property
But it was all in the plan
Captain John Pratt
Was the top cadet
In charge of the old military school when built
For all Indian children to be sent away from parents with no guilt
Cut their hair and forced to do daily chores
Punishment for speaking in their native tongue, scrubbing floors
Using a toothbrush to clean out toilets and the tiles
Parents lived away more than fifty miles
So many years away and later forgot their language they spoke
English was all they knew, one big hoax

Girls housework, boys hard labor
To work in the yards for their neighbor
'Curtis Act' cancelled out sovereignty, overriding treaties made
Land on reservations were shared with tribes, escapade
For the white settlers to get paid
U.S. government annuities
Not welfare or securities
Just a way to feed the Native American communities
Indians believed in the ghost dance to revive the dead
Had to be Christianized and all other spiritual thoughts out their head
Denoted the red
Indian leaders once said
They are not satanic practices or mental illness thoughts
It was only another scheme to get a piece of the land to be bought
When a man does not understand a culture, only fear
What they don't know, they desire it to disappear
Treaty rights were banned
Until Indians went to rallies and took a stand
The American Indian Movement fought
To share all their beliefs, language, and what they thought

Ideal of Life © 3/1993

Just a youngsta
Never imagined being a gangsta
From a Christian goodie-good-shoes teenager
Dreams of becoming a doctor, lawyer or professional
Everything started to fall
Downhill
Still
Attended college: Computer Engineering major
Then MIS until my junior
There was another lifestyle instilled in me: Early Childhood
To reach these kids, before committing suicide in their neighborhood
Income pay was too low
Changed major to Information Resources/Technology even though
I enjoyed working with the youth in the community as a volunteer
Did not do it for credit or cheer
Just to let the youth know that I am here
Those that felt mistreated, heated, and father cheated
Leaving you feeling used
Abused and accused
Of the entire incident
Something you did not commit
Years spent
Became bitter and unkempt
Since the day your father was sent to jail
With no bail
Every time the family goes to see him
Puts you through emotional hell
All the facial gestures and expresses tell
Making me want to yell
No critic
Stereotype trick
That made a switch
From the nice prissy role to the criminal role
Meeting some man, putting me in the hole
We never could get along
Some ding-dong
Had to move on
Throughout the relationships, my life seemed messed up
Someone always wanted to kick my butt
Assuming I'm real nice
Better think twice

Down that Road 5/21/2005

Do you swear it?
Repeating yourself like a parrot
Lies on the top of lies like Pinocchio
Watching your nose grow
Red as a pistachio
No echo
Hearing voices: Does that make you psycho?
Discreet
With this lustful heat
Hiding your car keys
Cheating like another dog with fleas
To pick up a female for a skeeze
To get on her knees
Fool please!
Lies of happiness and fortune
End up getting an abortion
With no solution
To the promises, soul left hollow
Who does she follow?
Can I trust again, to the extent of some belief
A memory of grief
A child she conceived
Now was retrieved
Dumped and thrown away
Ripped from the umbilical cord, others come today
Make me believe that you are the faithful type
Don't follow the hype
Don't lose your mind, tied up in white strips
Fall between the barrier
'Cause the road gets scarier
Unable to move out that layer
Of being a player-hater
All you want is to be an annihilator
Caught up in the storm
No one to keep you warm

This is a poem how one can lose their temper. Root of their money is evil. Promises are broken. Abortion is spoken in this poem; skeeze (today known as a 'jump-down' or 'holla-back') is referring to someone that has sex right away. Player haters—someone or people that envy the things you have. You shall not covet, 10th Commandment in the Holy Bible.

On the Prowl © 4/1994

Whose walking through all the smoke and the smog
The Devil and his co padres are the underdogs
Tougher than leather
Families unable to stay together
Children in group homes and foster care
Fear that no one will be there
Attitudes and emotions change like the weather
Anyone there when you need 'em
Homeless on the streets, can you feed 'em
Quit trying to pretend
Sleeping with your best friend
Lawyers defend
A father on the deep end
Attempted murder, not as crazy as Saddiam Hussen
High on cocaine
Elucidating seeing ghosts haunting you in the window pane
Practically going insane
A slow deadly killer
White dust in the system, gambling with a high wheeler
To dominate and control your body (and the world) like Hitler
Cracking up like Bette Midler
Constantly joking around like the Riddler
Fighting for your freedom, holding up your two fists
And later that night, slit your wrists
To stop hearing the voices, running the water hot
Staring at the picture hanging on your wall, school mascot
Stomach tied in a knot
Pressure and stress and bills due, put you on the spot
Feel there is no way to break loose or free
Once you die, only remain a memory
Death is your enemy
Eternal life is the true remedy

Suicide or Homicide © 3/28/2006

Thoughts of suicide
Observing Jesus dying on the Cross being crucified
After turning off the Passion of the Christ
Still thinking twice
Cannot let the bull slide
My passion hide
So petrified
All the emotions that linger inside
Pulled the trigger, another homicide

Thoughts of suicide
In this world all alone, unbelievable
Evilness on this earth can be deceivable
Matters incertitude
Dealing with people's attitude
No one I can include
Feelings allude
Knock the fool out with a bat, oh so crude
Thoughts of homicide
Holding the knife near my side
Or slit my throat, blood flows like a tide

Making moves, looking behind my back
Destroying the wack
Smoking on crack
Forgetting their kids and loved ones
What have I done?
Living in filth, no longer in charge
Drug habit is on large
Selling and dealing in my garage
White substances, pieces, is it a crack rock, only a mirage
Most of my life
Sucking on a pipe
Wearing my doo-rag
Willing to sell my flesh to get a stag
Foot drag
Pants sag
Overdose, turned into an old hag
Mood swings from Dr. Cheryl to Mrs. Hyde
Lost everything I had to pride
Thoughts of suicide
Or lying in the street dead, another homicide

Al 'Scar face' Capone Story © 5/1994

There were many criminal cases
Occurring in various places
A loan shark
Roaming the streets in the dark
Viciously stabbed sixty-three times by knives
This cat must have nine lives
Used an ice pick, strangled, and head crushed
Cheeks were blushed
Later he was rushed
To the hospital
Living felt impossible
No fairytale
A man short, snaky and pale
Life of a hustler and busted for a dope deal
Later known as the 'Big Tuna' from 1906 to 1992
Enforcer in Chicago for the Al Capone crew
Strapped with his machine gun
Fools did not hesitate to run
Left stunned
Hidden in his violin case
Swung a baseball bat upside a man's face
Beating down to death
Coughing up blood until his last grasp of breath
Pictures taken of this brutal scene
Show loyalty and courage was the routine
Joe Batters was his new nickname
It was an operation not a game
Joe was insane to the membrane
St. Valentine Day's massacre, still able to maintain
Listed as Public Enemy gang
Kidnapping 'Greasy Thumb' in 1945
Stayed out of jail using the 5th Amendment to stay alive
Chicago mafia in charge of enforcement
Frank Nitti ran the operations from then
Forced to retirement
Death was his experiment
Expired
Death was how one retired
1943 Nitti committed suicide
Death viewed as a homicide

Scar face II © 5/1994

Al Capone was responsible for all of this
In Chicago, crime was a bliss
Death with a kiss
What a way to reminiscence
Death only left silence
Capone was the most powerful and notorious gangster
Others represented as a prankster
Bootlegging whore houses, gambling
Liquor sampling
Joined Chicago Crime Syndicate at twenty-eight
Never had a real date
For brunch, had a head on his plate
Posted on Americas Most Wanted before age 33
America's most profitable business man of the century
Born in Brooklyn
Known as Crook-land
Only went up to the sixth-grade
Joined the five-point gang to get paid
Learned a new trade
That how it all begun
As the story continues on
Criminal association on the streets headed by John Torrio
Scar face became not only a legend but a hero
Got a scar from combat
Known for using the gat
Rat-tat-tat-tat
Killed over five hundred men and went to jail for income tax
Denied all the facts
Moved to Chi-town
Laying the law down
Scar face was his body guard, his aide was always around
1925 shot up in an ambush and barely survived
Thankful to be alive
Lead thirty million, retired, and gave it to Capone
Left in a syndicate all alone
His heart was cold and hard as stone
A popular figure of gangster heroes
Counting all their dinero (money)
1929, on Valentine's Day, in camouflage
Policemen entered in the garage
On North Clarke Street, target for 'bugs'
Up against the wall, gunned down by thugs
The Untouchables harassed Capone's mob for profit
Had to be a hit
Capone convicted and sentenced for eleven years
Looking up to by his peers

Capone Sega Ends © 5/1994

Capone suffered from untreated syphilis
Around his mouth and penis
Before penicillin was invented
This illness could have been prevented
Deteriorated by an alarming rate
Released from Alcatraz in 1939 to Miami Beach estate
From 1899-1947
Asking for mercy to God in heaven
Three brothers, James Capone, the oldest and boldest
Then Richard James 'Two-Gun' Hart
Had no part
In the gang violence from the start
Commander of Local American legion
Town Marshal, state sheriff in his region
Married, four sons, armed forces he was kicked out
Jobless and came to Al and died without a doubt
Frank was next in line
Worse than them all combined
Most vicious of them all
Watching men fall
On a death call
Frank had a more direct approach
Step on fools like a cockroach
Over disputes
Gun fires, it shoots
Who did not pay his loot?
No back talk from a dead corpse deceased
In a battle with the police
1895-1924, crime rate increased
Ralph 'Bottles' youngest enforcer
Married and divorced her
Drank liquor bottles and soft drinks
Wondering what a criminal thinks
Went to jail two years and four months in the joint
Income tax invasion, what is the point?
IRS spent thirty-five years to collect back taxes and other stuff
Confiscated two-hundred sixty-two vending machines, wasn't enough
100,000 packs of cigarettes and $7,500 in cash
Partial payment of $223 out of $294 of the stash
Interest and penalties by the cops and IRS
All the criminals had to confess
Not a story of the Wild, Wild West

On the Rough Side © 6/1994

Jessie James, Bonnie and Clyde
A life once lived and long died
Ruthless characters known for homicide
Rob and steal
Down for the kill
Anyone that squeals
Only doing it for thrills
Found dead
Shot in the head
Bleed
To death
Step to keep my rep
Watching a body drop
Cream of the crop
Blast the fool
Down to a molecule
Using skills, con-game
Able to tame
As I schooled ya
Fooled ya
Look at how I do ya
Rough, silent type
A hype strung out on the pipe
Ecstasy, giving you flavor
On my bad behavior
Finger on the trigger
In a split-second a dead ringer
Wisdom and money will prevail
Power and streets taught me well
Robbed open-handed
From some outlander bandit
Bag man collects money from the mob
Looking for a big man named Bob
Second-hand man in the neighborhood
Receiving money, mob up to no good
Paying off judges, lawyers, politicians and the police
Protection for their murderous and evasive crimes, no peace
Ruthless and nature is raw
Rebellious against the judicial law
Cold-blooded killers
Heartless, mean, big-time dealers
Hustlers and schemers, wheelers
No guidance to follow, reason to live

Love or hate, with nothing left to give
Struggle, heartbreak, and stress
Tired of all the mess
My life is not the best
Does the law always win?
Fade away by death are the wages of our sins

Guilty as Charged © 6/1994

Young boy refused
Anger was diffused
Holding a knife, confused
Sharp blade forced in the bedroom
Struggled with minor cuts, no sex was assumed
Fought, gagged on his breath
Fell unconscious, near death
Hired someone to beat up the boys
Additional charges added on the case
Other witnesses came forth at KFC place
Too embarrassed to show his face
Wife seduced, Gacy made her do sexual favors
To his next door neighbors
Served ten years in prison, wife divorced him and out of his life
Released in eighteen months, back to Chicago and got another wife
Women knew Gacy preferred boys
His wife didn't want to hear that noise
Sex and murder known as 'Pogo the Clown'
Cops continued to track him down
Sexual conflict
Less boys were tricked
Finding ways to capture 'em
Anything to get them
Homeless boys on the streets
Played as 'Detective Jack' in order to meet
Camouflage, so discreet
Boys playing the handcuff game
A mental illness, no one to blame
Hung by a rope
Hope, no longer could cope
He acted like he was on dope
Killed the boy and buried under the house, murders went on
Close surveillance to stop the killings, who was in the wrong?
For how long
December 21st, drug charge for marijuana in garage
He could not dodge
Thirty-five killings, charged for thirty-three
Pieces of flesh, skins and bones in buckets, still a mystery
Of what detectives had to see
Cords to strangle them to death or thrown in the river
Thoughts of the incident makes me quiver, shiver
March 1960 charged for life imprisonment
Was he guilty or innocent?

A Set-up © 6/1994

The commission
Was on a mission
Not connected
But stayed protected
Corrected
And well selected
To check all tabs
Busting caps
Playing craps
With finger snaps
Security system hooked up on the mansion
Roaming the streets looking for passion
Security check on the guys you meet
On the street
Heartless and restraint, feel the heat
Flames burst
Words cursed
Nothing rehearsed
Another reality show caused by body friction
From a drug addiction
Kicking it with my main man
Buying expensive things, asking for my hand
Big rock diamond instead of a gold wedding band
If I reply with a 'no' he won't understand
Organization got into a war with another mafia family
Going on for centuries
Hear no evil, see no evil, say no evil
Three Chinese monkeys
Bodies on freeze
Another overseas transaction, does not concern me
Honesty is how our relationship should be

Code of Silence © 3/28/2006

A code of silence
Seen enough violence
How could I be so hardcore?
Just to make a score
I did it all for love and a man I once adored
Living in the ghetto, so poor
What else could I do?
Who could I turn to?
The men were soldiers on guard
Windows and doors barred
No longer to be messed with
God granted me a gift
To watch this corpse body lay there stiff
Working a grave yard shift
One look
Is all it took
To get the man hooked
One smack in the head
Thought for sure I was dead
Seeing a light beam, gleaming red
Snipper
Marks on my body as if Jack the Ripper
Had done this damage to me
What stopped her?
The helicopter
Swarmed over our heads, then blew up in smoke
Now my life was in danger, no joke
After dark
Cops bordered at the park
No one took my side
Tears dried up as I once cried
All I could see
Was that my head was still bloody
Guilt over my face
Too late for the Lord to show me grace
What could I do?
With the man standing over me in blue
Officer placed the handcuffs on my wrists
A murder weapon that did not exist
Praying I did not kill the man I once seduced
What kind of crime did I produce?
My case was presented in front of a grand jury
Found guilty, felt like the 'Fist called Fury'

People continue to judge and make these type of decisions
To send me to prison
Murder for no apparent reason, without a cause
Whole life paused
Indicted
Set up to appear like an accident
That wasn't meant
In the apartment
To look 'Guilty before Proven Innocent'

A Set-back © 6/1994

Locked behind bars
Accused of manslaughter and stealing cars
Never did something illegal
Driving in BMW, Benz, and a Regal
In chains from hands to waist to feet
Forced in the courtroom to have a seat
Feeling of defeat
Jealousy and envious
Thoughts of being devious
Murder left me curious
To see a human being life taken
Broken into two and never awaken
Picture of a slut
Giving up my butt
Went to jail for what
To take the rap for this ho
That I didn't even know
Identity switched when I was drunk
To high to 'fake the funk'
She split
As I fought for the cops to quit
Wanted to be acquitted
Should I please insanity or tell the real deal
Think I had the motive to kill
Still
I would not do something totally against my will
My main trick bailed me out of jail
Left me at the house to sell
Cops busted in without a search warrant for a drug bust
Reading the dollar bill, 'In God we trust'
Innocent bystander as I bit the dust
Thrown to the floor
Handcuffed me from the back on top of me like I was a whore
What the heck are you doing this for?
Read me my rights, found with narcotics
Planted there
Claimed I had it everywhere
Sent down to the police station
For this situation
More counts against me since I was on probation
No bail, no parole
Judge wanted to see me rot in this hole
Charged with murder from the first-degree

Attempted to explain all this to the attorney
But it was really up to the jury
A capital offense
Appeared to be dense
To the facts
Planned out just an act
To bring down the black
Thought I was lying through my crooked teeth
Whole night I could not sleep
Counting sheep
No Bo Peep
Idea of who had done it
Made the pieces fit
To get laid
Avoided to get sprayed
Whole masquerade
Knew how much money he made
Counting all the money and how much it will take
Committed the crimes while I wasn't awake
Thank God I was not shot
Money tied up in a knot
In the process
For sweet success
Anyone got in her way
Buried their bodies to decay
Boyfriend visited me in the cell
Eyes red like flaming fire in Hell
Money making
Money taking
No faking
Leaving my man heart-breaking
Stomach churning
Yearning for a six-figure earning
Men is who she is burning
Cash flowing
Jealousy showing
Continue hoeing
No circumstantial evidence
Whole incident was non-sense

Deception and Intention © 6/1994
(Virginia Hill 1918-1966)

Men happened to fall in love with her
From mafia, stealing to dealing, and then committing murder
Bugsy seen a beautiful, smart, capable female
Ultimate lover and able to handle deals which no one could tell
A woman emotions guarded in a hard shell
Taking Bugsy money when all things failed
Virginia was the bag lady of an organized crime
Various skills, paid and served no time
There was a movie about him and her life
Mistress that removed him from his kids and wife
Got the nickname at sixteen, "the Flamingo"
Bugsy named the casino in Reno
In Las Vegas, under Virginia's name
People were suspicious on how she played her game
Three times a lady
Every man asking her to have their baby
Things got shady
One fly female
Body with much detail
Loose ends
No friends
Who need them, she ran her scam
Making suckers point out who I am
Taking all his dough
Like he did not know
A well-rounded ho
Cashed it all and heart cut out
Even though this was not what she was about
It appeared that no one understood
Investing money on the casino project did good
A dancer in 1934 in Chicago World Fair
As men dropped their tongues and stared
What a beauty with a body and the way she wore her hair
Bout a home in LA, on trips
Men paid to get between those hips
Skinny dip
'I'm the best in the world' she quoted
March 1966 in Austria was overdosed on sleeping pills, papers wrote
And left no note

Stories of Alcatraz © *6/1994*

Alcatraz is an island on San Francisco Bay
Where hardcore criminals have to pay
For their debts to society for their horrible crimes
During depression, sign of the times
1865, U.S. War Department had a prison for deserters in the military
Quite on the contrary
Buried in your own cemetery
Worse than the penitentiary
1933, was named the 'super-prison for super-criminals of the century'
Now it's just a dreadful memory
Escape proof
From the floors to the roof
More than what any prisoner had in store
So much water to swim ashore
Handcuffed to cell bars was painful
Beaten down to the skull
Scared in the darkness, brutally abused
To serve time and pay their dues
A life no man would choose
Throw away the key, locked up for life, you loose
Watered down by hoses, tied up in a straight-jacket
Food and clothes hacked
All the drama between inmates and the racket
A hole on confinement
Horrible and terrifying place to be spent
From Al Capone, George "Machine Gun" Kelly
From murder, extortion, and felony
Arthur "Dock" Barker, Alvin "Creepy" Karpis to name a few
'Birdman of Alcatraz', a story that was so true
Discussions about the bird disease and things they would do
Inside the hole
Big time hustlers and fools that stole
Never on bail or on parole

A Crime to be Black © 4/1994

A race war
What for?
Got the statement wrong, saying I was trying to be hardcore
Lost in the wilderness
Being on a pedestal
Believing 'white is right', this is a radical
Whose pulling the trigger on the pistol
Series of racial incidents inexcusable accidents
Promises of your predictions
Stories are said to be fiction
Get us hooked on drugs and alcohol is an addiction
Your politics is just to get your kicks
Portraying us to be maids and whores on your movie flicks
Thought makes me sick
Like putting a nine-millimeter to my head
Praying that we are all dead
A half breed fed up
Time to let up
Your hopes of unity
Destroying my community
With these political issues, really a scheme to get paid
Riches from the strength of our hands as our women laid
How do blacks and white get along?
Separated from our country, land, and language, how do we belong?
We have grown strong
In some things, unable to go back to Africa our motherland
Too late to fully understand
Still living in slave mentality
Just using a different strategy
Been in America too long
Singing the same ole song
White man this, white man that
You need to do more than say, cuz I'm black
Whose the real enemy
Trying to find a remedy
To the problem like Abraham Lincoln and John F. Kennedy
No one was able to speak
Until Martin Luther King
Let freedom ring
Today, many are too weak
To reach others to that peak
As brothers killing brothers, laid out in a creek
So rotten

To be a real hero and long forgotten
What are we dealing with
To have life is a gift
Color made people shift
To being white, something I can never be
Just take one good look at me
It is obvious to see
High yellow tone
Neither race do I truly belong
What is the reaction?
Across the nation, still dealing with some form of segregation

Crime to Be Black II © 4/1994

In the past, watching Negroes get splattered
Some based on chit-chatter
What is the matter?
Old testimonies and slave movies, seeing us die
Lord, did you hear our cry?
We were in bondage for over 400 years
I keep on wondering why
Did we suffer?
Did we learn to love one another?
Did we learn to love our enemies regardless of our situation?
We were free around 1865 under emancipation
Arizona could not accept M.L. King Holiday
King risked his life to pave the way
Believed in non-violence
Today, there is still no real peace or silence
From all the negative and prejudice noise
Klu Klux Klan and rednecks boys
Gun shots blasting
Deaths everlasting
Lost all determination and ambition
Even in the 21st century, still unable to make your own decisions
Reflecting back to the slave mentality
You need to face your own reality
Deal with your own issue
Respect others point of view
Maybe someone would want to hear you
Study and read about historical figures and great men
But when
Will other races give in
So many of us are mixed, bi-racial, or other cultures
Stop destroying us like vultures
Referring to the Bible for your cruelty
Scriptures to explain your duty
God is love--He would not allow such an act to happen
So we all need to quit snappin'

Make a Difference © 4/1994

No one is making a difference to preserve
Our heritage, culture, and artistic figurines we could conserve
Always have to get up the nerve
To run away from racism and other types of fear
Preach to each
And teach
Our children our history for those we can reach
Stand on our own ground
African Americans locked up in the pound
Or dead from messing around
There appears to be something or someone to bring us down
Forgot about our Civil Rights
Many of us killed in fights
437 years ago, violence was done
How come
Don't let anyone call you ignorant or dumb
For too long and too many suffered to lose our establishment
Don't let it be a disappointment
All this crap started from the government
To govern our lives and laws to justify
Now we have to look at the emancipation to make sure it was not a lie
Rules changes in 2006 or 2007
Abraham Lincoln wanted justice and peace to enter the gateways of heaven
To win the hearts and minds of all people
We should treat each other as an equal
Even though it happened centuries ago
Some feel it is hard to let go
Lost from our roots and its true meaning
Started in Egypt, enslavement, 400 years of bondage in the beginning
Can be found in Exodus, the Bible
Moses separated the Red Sea on God's call to avoid a rival
In the wilderness, ate manna, and followed God's rules for survival
Israelites did not appreciate it one bit
Missed the Promised Land, love has a lot to do with it
Black and Indian heroes died violently
These stories are hid silently
Some fights lead to revolution
So many leaders tried to come to a solution
Now we have crimes, deaths, and prostitution
One huge pollution to believe in evolution
N.W.A. rapped, 'Forget the Police'
Where is the peace?
Crimes doesn't appear to cease
Is it due to the baby boomers, such an increase?
Or people doing what ever it takes to survive
To stay alive!

The Unborn Child © 4/17/2006

After the conception
A sensation indescribable
Start to feel indifferent
Embryo, small living creature
In my womb
Imagining what the birth experience will be like
Life-threatening, complications, or something wrong with the baby
Birth defects, Lord, please let the child be normal
Healthy, boy, girl, twins, triplets, who knows
As the embryo grows
What I eat, drink, it feeds this seed
The seed that my mate planted
In my womb
I cannot wait to see the child bloom
From my uterus, my vagina
To see its head, praying it does not come out feet first
Breech birth, cesarean, or through the tunnel
Baby, blood and mucus, and placenta gush out the funnel
The pain, dang, the pain
Tears flow like rain
Partner is not there
Claiming it is not his
What a nightmare!
Wake up, seeing my soul mate there
Whoa, this man cares!
He watches our child come out the hole
Nearly faints, as I lose control
Nails clinch in his hand, bleeding and screaming
Will you let go!
You have this darn baby
Just a dream, since I am on the cold steel table
Legs open, feet on a silver clutch
Doctor pressing
Legs stressing
Until he sucks the life out of me
Lifeless embryo in a glass jar
To be thrown away from this misery, pain, and suffering
I could not bare to bring life in this world
Not now at least
God forgive me, I am a beast
To see this embryo, lifeless and will be thrown in the trash
Full of pride like King Nebuchadnezzar, eating grass
Lord, you forgive your children, I know I am forgiven
Is it worth living?

Trick that Switched © 6/1997

The trick that switched
Once she got a taste
Our friendship was a waste
Thought we were cool at first
Later things got worse
Held my feelings in too long
So many derogatory things I wanted to burst
Out of my mouth, she was a phony
Now I am left lonely
She acted like she owned me
Wish she had never known me
Never was a true homey
Once I seen your true self, you reminded me of a heifer
Every man in his right mind left her
She will push every button
Actually over nothing
Her evil motives are so hideous
Hard to take her serious
Almost went delirious
Imagined you were snorting coke
Since you were always so broke
But never even seen you smoke
Yet you laughed at everything as if it was a joke
After our conflict, I never wanted to be in the same room
Studied more than you assumed
On campus, many would ask me
If you were nasty
Doing favors
Messing around with your neighbors
But I was not involved in that freaky behavior
I lived for the true Savior

This is a True Story about a colleague attending at Milwaukee School of Engineering (Vanessa). I believed she was older and could be a mentor to me while sharing a campus dorm with her, but things changed quickly.

Girl I thought I knew © 6/1997

Grades starting falling
You kept constantly calling
Asked friends for their help
Knew you were only out for self
I shared things with you that I felt
Bills we still did not deal with
Pissed off about the phone bill
True feelings came out for real
Your man looked like a fag
Only show and tell, always tried to brag
You appeared to be an old hag
As your clothes sagged
Associates for awhile
Getting hostile
Need to change your attitude and whole style
Saw you as another hoochie
Giving up the couchie
Hygiene is important and needed to douche
Bit of advice
It was a sacrifice
To be nice
Time for some action
Started to dislike you with a passion
Kept asking
To pretend that we were never friends
Only wanted this arguments to come to an end
Became like the little rascal
Everything with you became a hassle
Not here to offend
What you needed to comprehend
You were 22 and I was 18, wanting me to lend
You monies for the phone
But you showed all the long distance on the bill alone
I moved out to a single room in a suite to leave you on your own
Funny how you claimed to be grown

❄

This is a true story of how a roommate (Vanessa) on campus made me feel
after we had a dispute over a phone bill that was not even in her name.

❄❄

Major Trial © 6/1997

I did not want our relationship to end this way
Crime does not pay
All I could do was pray
For what you have done to us on that day
Could never forget
Easy to forgive but regret
Losing a father that I loved, heard nothing yet
About why you did it
Need to admit it
No more excuses, tell me the truth
Took away my youth
Grew up at a quick age
Hate to see you locked up behind a cage
Treated with cruelty, arrested
God's love manifested tested
To make you a believer of His power
To that last hour
Not sure what triggered you off, how it all begun
Warrant for your arrest, out on the run
Caught at the home
Watched television and all alone
Strange calls on our telephone
Argued over silly stuff, hit me first
Started to cuss, fuss, things got worse
Ducked back
Talked more crap
Full of rage to attack
Kicked you off of me, sister got in the way
Scared for my life, reminiscence on that day
Stayed in an overnight shelter
Felt like helter skelter
Out at night, no molester
No job, daily looking
Out on Bailey Avenue, not down for hooking
Only thoughts of you
Had to take the bus to Juan's house, thought we were through
God blessed us with the things we needed
To go on with our lives to succeed
The past
Cut by glass
Happened to fast
Love shall last
Father became abusive

Story in Riverside, CA exclusive
Once we left
You will never know how we felt
Tons of questions, millions of times
Did you suffer for the crime?
No matter how mad
You are still our dad
Learn to calm your temper
Came back in September
Drama started the end of December
Had fun before the damage was done
January 4th, guy busted through patio glass
January 8th when the whole world clashed
Dad cooked a big meal
True emotions, red eyes revealed
Thought to kill
Something hit your intensity
Kicked in sensitivity
Lost control of reality
Yelling for help
Just my sister and myself
Called 9-11, blood everywhere
No one in the apartment complex cared
We were unprepared
Both of us were scared
Emotions ride
Anger and pride
Drinking Cisco these feeling could not hide
Took the anger out on us
Now we all pray to Jesus
We can love again and mend our past
And be able to love and forgive, relationship that will last

This happened back in January 1994 while living with our father in Riverside, CA. We thought our dad was going to slice my neck with a broken Coke glass, later they came to arrest him and took my sister to the hospital in the ambulance. Then, we had to undergo interrogation from the D.A. office to determine his jail sentence.

On Trial © 6/1997

So many things stirred up in my mind
About a past I tried to leave behind
Rewind and played over and over again
As the trial begin
Enemies appeared as your own kin
Started with my own father
Drinking Cisco, not in the mood to be bothered
Talk of being a doctor, he desired to be
Blames my mother for having me
After two kids, his dreams became a misery
No excuse for the abuse
What's the use
To hit her
But you still miss her
As you continue to diss her
Smokes and drinks too much
No longer able to keep in touch
Fought my mom down while she was butt-naked
A thought came in my head for a second
But you wrecked it
Human bites on her back, bloody mouth and broke jaw
Then one day you left my sis with scar on her face, against the law
To hit on a minor
Your daughter could not wear eyeliner
Or seen in a diner
Her eyes had to heal from the redness
Everyone asked who done this
Come to Cali for a place of happiness
To feel blessed
But you drank
Breath stank
As your mind went blank
Fell on the floor
Yelling to lift you up to walk to the door
And buy some more
Liquor figure
That you would argue even quicker
Then seen you hit her
Called our mom long distance
Resistance from your presence
Attempted to leave
Grabbed me and then a fist, hard to believe
From all the love I once received

That you could hurt me with such muscles under your sleeve
Broke the Coke Cola glass on the bed
Ready to aim for my head
Lay flat across the mattress
Fully dressed
Distressed from all the non-sense
Threatened to slash my throat
From the same Coke Cola glass you broke
Never lost my faith and hope
Guess you snapped cracked
Or a life style of raising daughter you could not adapt
Lost your dreams and unable to fulfill your destiny
Almost got the best of me
The oldest, it was so hard
Fighting and yelling heard through the courtyard
At one time, I grew up raising other kids
No matter what I did
You cried and hid
Behind your feelings when your kids came
We was part of the blame
For all your shame
Hard to believe the entire incident
Was simply an accident
Was your intentions really meant?
Nightmare I dreaded to know the truth
Did it start during your youth?
You were the oldest too
Cleaning, raising kids, and other things I had no clue
You fled from child support
Years ago in court
Ran to New York
On trial for awhile
No sympathy, not even a smile
Tears fell
My sister and I thought we knew you well
Who can tell
Until everything fails

Past memory back in January 1994 in Riverside, CA. We have reunited and renewed our relationship with our father. He is our best friend, father, and mentor. He helps us when we need him most in our adult years, but we have forgiven and put the past behind us. Families can reunite with the grace and love of God.

Comedic Poem Selection

What U should know (can hurt) © 10/2/2005

Keep your words clean
Like good hygiene
Breath kicking, use Listerine
Or use some Dentine
Saw you with your homey at the house par-tay (party)
Showing your bod-ay (body)
Getting all naugh-tay (naughty)
No jay
Could make you act this way
Must be a natural high
Flying high like the birds in the sky
Saying you are a true blue
But you had no clue
Wishing you knew
What you want to do
Followed after a crew
Guns fired, you scared to death, pants full of doo-doo
Boo-hoo
Where is your crew?
At the club
Smoked your dub
When you could have sold your stash
For some cash
Rest on some loving
Start rubbing
Undress this female
Cross-dressed, turned out to be a male
Can you escape?
Too late, on video tape
Copies sold to your boys
Can't hang with the real McCoy's
Kill that noise...
Blown out of proportion Extortion
Trying to keep up my composure
Under such pressure
Dang, I am out the gang for sure
Boy, did I not score
With the cross-dressed whore!
Beauty is only skin deep, not what I had in store
Won't go out like that anymore...
Check the Adam's apple
Crack that fool open like Snapple
Won this maiden from a contest raffle

Just another Tune © 3/1994

Turning on the radio
While riding in my SUV, finding somewhere to go
Switch up on day two
Listening to Snoop
In the Deville Coup
Down to chill
For real
Called my guy on the cell phone
To stop at the house to get it on
Beeper lighting up
So what
Switching my hips with my Toni Braxton, Halle Berry short hair cut
Fellas staring at the butt
Only will call back the ones worth my time
Not messing around with the swine
Wine on their mind
To feel all over this big behind
Oh my my my
Singing, 'aint nothing wrong with a little bump and grind'
Trying to change my mind
R Kelly sex moods, maxing back to the slow jams
Drifting into a sexual desire, forgetting who I am
Getting busy with my main man
My body is calling, sex me, playback rewind
Watching this fool get buck-wild
That ain't my style
From the behind
Dang, this man is driving me wild
Pulling on my hair like I am his step-child
He won't quit
House music to gangster rap, pass me a splint
Half-lit
Now they up in the house having a fit
Putting on the oldies hits
To the Bone Thugs N Harmony
Asking the brother what is his symphony
Just in case we take this to another level
One minute an angel, next minute a Devil
Glazed in his face
As I turn up the bass
This brother was a total waste
Once I had to put him in his place
Just another tune up in your face

Drama for your mama © 3/1994

After all the drama I have been through
Pulling out my hair, asking what is I going to do?
Avoiding the negativity when I am with my crew
Dang, his breath smells like doo-doo
What did he brush his teeth with?
Boy that odor is not a gift
Got this sister standing like a stiff
Wondering what is wrong with me
Lord, have mercy
And give him a tic-tac
Instead I walk away and he only stares at my back
Was I so wrong
Well hear me say, 'so long'
No hood set I'm claiming
Just saying
True blue
Thought you knew
Color I like to wear
Really don't care
About this GD, Disciples, gangster mentality
Or Crip and Blood, let's face reality
Folks and peoples sound like peeps we hang out and kick it
Crip sounds like R.I.P.
Blood that flows through our veins or Jesus Christ blood dripped
From his head
As he cried to the Lord, before he was dead
Blood of Christ is who and what we should represent
Since it brings life from the past to the present
It is your choice to your lifestyle
During Judgment, don't sing, 'Let's wait awhile'
When you have a chance to change your attitude and style
Or find yourself on top of lost souls at the peak of the pile
Don't be ashamed
Don't point the finger, no one is the blame
Nothing just playing the Adam and Eve blame-game

Out to get Deez © 3/1994

The party started
The stiffness stayed
In the air after someone farted
But everyone still hung around
As friends started to clown
Nothing seemed to matter once I saw you standing there
Imagining you walking inside the place, bare
No hair
No clothes on, trying not to stare
I could only be dreaming
Music streaming
Fools stepping, ready to jack
Guns pulled out, not knowing how to act
Feeling myself about to snap
Karate, kung-fu, up in the spot
Matrix moves, footwork getting hot
A gang thang
Throwing fists and guns in the air, yanking out their ding-a-ling
Boy, look at those balls hang
Only dreamed of you like this
As the shots blew in the mist
As you feel on top of me with a juicy moist kiss
The bullets in the air missed
The both of us
Other ran, burning dust
My thoughts through all this was on lust
It is a must
As your muscles start to bust
Out of that whitey
Smitey
Can't take things lightly
Watching him fight for me
I opened my mouth
Exposed my thoughts out
To let you know what I am really all about
Your chest
Against my breast
I have to confess
I would love to put that body to the test
As I lay down to rest

Lost in a fantasy at a party © 3/1994

The party was banned
I could barely stand
Listening to the one eye band
At the moment
I thought you were God scent
As you flew in my arms, running scared, hallucinating
Concentrating
On making it safe and sound in my home
But too scared to stay alone
This guy promised to walk me there safely, only an illusion
Trapped in my own confusion
Continue to wonder if you care or feel the same
I know you do once my name ends with your surname
I had to keep my cool
Spit slipped from my lips and started to drool
Laying on my pillow
Looking out the window
I knew that I would be the last time I will ever see you again
Only attracted to me as a friend
The thought made my heart drop
Could not stop
Thinking of you my love
Staring at the stars and clouds above
What is my purpose here?
A life living in fear
Almost near death, will I go to Heaven or Hell
No one can tell
Noticing the wart swell
Boy, did it smell
Whether I will be in school or end up in jail
Kicking it with my crew
Finally stopped reminiscing on you
With totally nothing to do
Walking to the corner store to see you

Kicking the Low-Down © 5/1994

Oh men, oh men, your princess is here
Abbra caddbra she shall appear
A female of your wildest dreams
Storming through the atmosphere
Pounding down with a thousand tons of exploding rhymes
Drop the bomb, breaking dollars into dimes
Powerful vocals to overcome the sign of times
Proud of who I am
What player-haters have to say, I don't give a damn
Just that tricks better stay off my man
Want to succeed in hooking him, only I can
Continue to give him clues, winking my eye
As you stroll by
Don't pretend to be so innocent and shy
Cause you will end up looking like Popeye
Never trust a girl around him
Martial affairs and life seems so blim
Sleeping with kin
Giggling, this is no joke
Especially when you are dead broke
Gagging on a chicken bone, start to choke
Always blaming the man, may be true in some case
But not when you know the situation and your booty all in his face

Buck Wild © 3/28/2006

Dang, he wants to get buck wild
Don't treat me like your step-child
Do you love me truly
Or just all up on the bootie
My hormones on overload
Hot, oh rub that spot, oops not that bold
Wrong hole
Especially when it is hard as a flag-pole
Nectar makes you loose and out of control
As my flaps unfolds
Kicking and moving his flow harder than your father
Weak rappers don't even bother
Up and down like a yo-yo
The D to the E ending with an O
Stealing the show
Not your ho
Not impressed
Do I need to stress
I could not be treated like some trick
All up on your d...
What apple did you pick?
From the good batch or bad
So arrogant and speaking about what you had
Standing around for my autograph
Then told your story in the National Inquirer
What attorney did you hire?
Only seeking a fix
Cocaine addict traveled from Chicago to Phoenix
Backstage as a groupie with superstars performing a trick
Teaser skeezer
Expecting life to be easier
Out for a real man to please her
Want to get high
Tracks on the arms, different way to die
A desire unable to satisfy
Life goes bye-bye

1 Knock, 2 Knock, 3 Knock © 4/17/2006

1 knock, 2 knock, 3 knock
I peep through my keyhole
Some guy from down the block

1 knock, 2 knock, 3 knock
This guy was a cutie
Feeling all on my booty
While on duty
A cop on 53rd block

1 knock, 2 knock, 3 knock
Who is knocking on my door at this hour
It was time for me to retire
Open the door to glare at the Jehovah Witness flock

1 knock, 2 knock, 3 knock
I thought this flock came back
Open the door to find some guy high off crack rock
Slapped the door shut
Last sound I heard, was him flapping down on his butt
What a runt!

1 knock, 2 knock, 3 knock
Banging on my door
I run to see who it could be
It is my financial advisor to speak about my stock
Making millions, man I rock!

1 knock, 2 knock, 3 knock
I cannot wait, anticipate for my lover
Knock the boots off and makes me kick off my socks
Good loving, here and there
Man, I am all up on his jock!

Need Space for this Face © 6/1997

Salt N Pepa gave you hot and vicious
X-ta$y is so sweet and delicious
Mysterious curious
How a female can be so serious
No comparison to Yo-Yo
Can feel Deo flow
Through your stereo
No sell-out, or sell her body to schemers
Some people are only dreamers
Deo is a true believer
As your guy is on the receiver
Phone being tapped
Did your girl snap?
Over a piece of crack
Homey was jacked
From not watching his back
Some people do not know how to act
Under attack
Diminish
Career is finished
Shined your head across the concrete like shoe polish
Demolish
You are dismissed, go!
Pimping your ho
Oh no, act like you don't know
All you can come back with is "so!"
Man hollers my name with no shame
As I continue to kick game
Pronounced D-E-O
Sister with an ego
But ain't free though
Cant play me like no dough-dough
Cypress Hill the phunky feel
Babyface with whip-a-peel
And X-ta$y with sex-appeal
Pimp ya flip ya still hit ya
Slashed in half
As I crack a smile and laugh
Say that your out to kill
All in my grill
Just chill
Or I will have to get ill for real
Keep your girl on the pill

Ice Cube said "Really doe"
As Deo keeps it mellow
Hardcore to romantically slow
Flashy cars and know that their still poor
Pleading for more
Mo' money mo' money mo' money
As the next man pimps ya like a dummy
Pimp mac takes no slack
For those on Prozac
Can you comprehend apprehend
Fornication is a sin
Drain our all possessions
Driven by obsessions
Taught a dear lesson
Keeping your partner guessing
This good-loving, screaming hallelujah
See what through ya
Can you hang?
With this g-thang
Bring in the Big Bang (New Year)
All on your ding-a-ling
Your boys can sing
What can you bring?

Sweet as U can be © 6/1997

Sweet like skittles
As I flow this riddle
Fiddle
Faddle
Sound hitting harder than a rattle
Breaking through like an earthquake
Born into this world, no mistake
To keep watching others come off fake
Too proud to beg
Playing women with your third leg
What a stag!
Turned out to be a fag
What a drag!
Your old hag acting like she is on her rag
On her neck hangs soldier's tags
Rocking the gold lynx
What you think?
Claim your stuff doesn't stink
Blink, so pretty in pink
It makes me sick
To see those older fellows wink
Wearing tight spandex
Brand X
Covered with latex

Miscellaneous & Hardcore
Poems Section

Hard Times © 6/1/1997

Parents get hysterical
Praying for a miracle
So petrified
No matter how hard they've tried
We never get by
The hard times as I see my mother cry
Can't benefit
By being illiterate
Hard to find a decent job to work
Pops is going berserk
Because dad feels that life is so complicated
Full of hatred
People are scared
Dared
Have to come prepared
For things to come
Growing up in the slums
Around bums
Searching for bread crumbs
Cry
Or shall I die
The pain I felt inside
People do dirt for dirt
Someone will get hurt
During the winter storm
Trying to stay warm
No heat was on during the blizzard
Eating on chicken gizzard
Dreams of being naked
Can get shot in a split second
Obscene
In a magazine
Writing stories that are unclean
Publicize
Criticize
A person that I don't even recognize

On the Chase © 4/1994

Full grown
Alone
Nightmares, hard to sleep
Pray to the Lord my soul to keep
My man on the creep
Singing outside my window with harmony
This mystery man continued to watch me on the balcony
Symphony
Music played by the bands in the streets, but my spirit is still empty
Feeling so lonely
Most people are phony
In my mind, my guy was just a homey
Subconsciously unspoken
He thought I was jokin'
Like I've been smoking'
No drugs in my system
He would not listen
Assumed I would diss him
Caught the next airplane
Tears feel like the rain
Elevate
Deflate
To his fate
Broken him in half like a decimal
Unquestionable
Dastard
So smooth, that bastard
He had me fooled
Schooled
To use his tools
Fool lost his screws
'Lady sings the blues'
Distill
Popped my birth control pill
Took a peek
Been over a week
Memories of love-making at the creek
It was late, blood drip
How did he slip?
Can't be true, got to get a grip

Betrayed © 11/04

Been betrayed
To get paid
Have to open minded
Mislead or blinded
By people that act like they're cool
Making me out for a fool
Another advocate
That's trying to make it
Looking for a gig
To be big
But I got overboard
Pulled a muscle in my vocal chord
While I was on tour
A disaster not an encore
A feeling, I allured
As my fans begged for more
Beautify my talent across the stage
Surrender to all demands, outraged
Treat me like an animal locked in a cage
Not able to justify
Only my tears purify
I be-rate
What one will generate
As I demonstrate
What I am capable of doing
Without screwing
Never was petite
My personality is bittersweet
One you can not compete
When you see me on the street
Playing black jack in Vegas
Kids are entertained by Sega's
Will I betray
Anyone that takes my pay
Do you notice the delay?
In what I say
When I have you believing that everything is okay
As the money is astronomical
My performance was phenomenal
Blessed by what God has manifest
Can attest
That God is the best

Guilty Before Proven Innocent (G.B.P.I.) © 12/1992

As I begin to rap
I'm going to take it way back
The days when people use to party
Drinking beer, wine, and Bacardi
No hard feelings no arguments
People was kind, little things that started a fight
People did not pay any mind
Church girl and very educated
My family and peers hated it
Decided to change my whole appearance and lifestyle
Started hanging with my peers and drinking and getting wild
Met a guy gang banging
Slanging
Wonder what is up with that
Always watching my back
Met a guy running from the cops or the gang members
Locked behind bars, a nightmare he'll always remember
Living a criminal life
Carrying a weapon—gun or knife
Ready to fight
For his boys or his hood
Something that I never understood
No cure for all the gang banging
Dope dealing
And all the killing
Just another victim
Down to search him
With a gun
No where to run
Cops asking what has he done
A juvenile delinquent
Spent
Time in a cell
With crazy criminal stories to tell
A convict
In a conflict
With the law and trying to get away real quick
Can't walk the streets without getting stopped
By a cop
Once he was caught
He fought
And was brought
To court, boys in the black and blue

Handcuffed him for something he didn't do
A bystander at the scene of the crime
At the wrong place and at the wrong time
Fitting the given description
Sent to detention hall
Only allowed to make one phone call
A teen
At the age of sixteen
Followed the wrong path
Grasp
With the rest of his life to look back and laugh
Black men don't know who to turn to
Or what to do
Grew up the hard way
With no food or place to stay
Grew up in a dysfunctional and corruptive homes
Seeing people get shot in the dome
Parents leaving them all alone
Alcoholic father beating on the mother
No one can do a darn thing but push it undercover
Life is a living hell
How much can one compel?
Locked in a cell
Too many young brothers going to jail
Every time you turn on the news
Whose
The next black man
How much cans one stand?
Say "Give a helping hand?"
No one is standing up to help
While the white man lives in wealth
Thrown in jail, treated like a wild beast
Misconception needs to cease
Crimes and death has increased
We need more peace

This is a song that was written when I was 18. I met this juvenile male, Juan, that felt he was trapped in the ghetto with only gangster tactics to survive; the only life he has known living in San Bernardino, CA. Later, it deals with scenes of the police, jail (detention) and gangster mortality when he was 16-17 and the misconceptions of a black man.

So Low, where can I go? © 5/20/2005

There are a low percentage of men
Even lower percentage of blacks
Yet, most of these black men don't know how to act
Either got a big ego, willing to die over dope or cash
Caught by the cops and located their stash
Locked in jail or dead
There is a price for your head
Still trying to adapt
So I decided to rap
That the system is wack
While some believe that the white man owns everything
"Let Freedom Ring"
Is that slavery mentality?
Got to face reality
What you doing for me?
Time to do our own thing
To make freedom ring
Look at Halle Berry winning a Grammy
Not playing someone's Mammy
Rap artists and other music performers doing it
Violence will only ruin it
Expose us on television live
How will this race survive?
So much mixture
Is anyone pure?
To feel accepted
Just deal with it
Only I felt it
Told to be a brilliant child
That went a little wild
Having men on the side, changing my style
When I was grown
I realized I was on my own
Torn
Between parents, having to choose
Either way I would loose
Mom or dad
This situation made me feel bad
How could they put you in a situation like that, so sad
Divorce is the cause
How marriage and Jesus Christ in relationships are lost
Put everything on pause
Push play, no sympathy or help

As I wept
No one to truly know how I felt
Enduring the pain of the belt
So I took the paper and pen
Started to write
To express the way my heart and mind felt
When I was the age ten
Way back then
No one to turn to
Needing money or a place to stay, who
Will help you
When things seem no way through
No reason to point the finger
As your misery, depression, and pain linger
Who's the real nigger?
How you figure?
Do you know the meaning?
Then, why are we calling each other that slave name?
Man, our race is going insane
Need to figure out our past, slave mentality, to remain!

This poem is an overlook on how life can be or turn out for our youngsters by seeing their parents fighting, fussing, and divorce one another. I was a child that witnessed her parents fussing and ended up in divorce court. We need to know our past to move forward. We need to find ourselves, true selves, not trying to be someone we are not! We need to find Jesus Christ! Certain parts of the poem above are true experiences about my life and how many of us still have the slave mentality.

Parents Trippin © 5/20/2005

Parents tend to complain
I did not cause this strain
This sorrow and some of this pain
I was not asked to be born in this world
I am just your little girl
As you cuss me out and yell
Until there was nothing more to tell
Wish your problems that you're going through--mom, would disappear
Once adulthood comes near
I will no longer be a burden in your life, no longer here
No need to fear
Once I step through the campus doors
A moment you should adore
Graduation
All I want to hear is congratulations!
Moms, said she went through a life of prostitution
Pops dope dealing and stealing, what caused this situation?
You sleeping with any man to get that feeling
Stimulation, demonstrating to understand how you are wheeling
That cash and still love my dad, in my subconscious mind
Still trying to find
Who I am or who I will be, leaving these incidents behind
Have to clear my mind
Survive off of food and need shelter
From the weather
Wish our family could stay together
All I did was runaway, but did not make the problems better
My mom gave me a hint
That it is no fun being pregnant
Especially as a teen mother
What happened to my black brother
My man, my boo, the one that shared what we went through
Dodge me for another
Skank what he thank
I will smother
Love him like no other
Stole a part of me I cannot get back
Should I slash those tires and attack
Watching him live in her mansion
While I am still struggling and living in this shack
Should I have this child or give it away
Hoping for a better day
Hopefully I can give this child a better place to stay

Dang, you still remain in my heart
Once we departed
Looking back down memory lane to see how it all started
Don't want to take it to my father
Why bother?
Now you find the wrong time
To say the child isn't mines
Because you think I am with some swine
All up on the behind
Man, you are out of line
Did you lose your dang ole mind?
Too late to come back into my life
Choose someone else to make your wife!

This poem is about the struggles of being a parent. Parents are able to see their daughter, following their footsteps and watch their daughter struggle too. Break the cycle: teen parents. Break the cycle: men not standing up to be fathers won't even bother, saying the 'child is not mines'. And then when a man sees his ex woman happy, he wants to come in and interfere.

This poem comes from the song, 'Ideal of Life', revised and updated.

Hard As Ever © 8/1993

Don't talk crazy while I'm standing
Commanding
Keep it up, you'll be landing
On yo' butt
Now what's up
Walking, strolling down the wrong path
Not in the mood to laugh
Take time to sign an autograph
Smooth mc
Light n lovely
Sexy but don't test me
May look good
Down for mines, lift up the car hood
Until I am fully understood
Don't give me that coulda-woulda-shoulda
Oh crap
I have to adapt
Or I will have to snap
Things get hazy
But I try not to let things phase me
Or you will end up crazy
Don't get caught walking in a dark alley
Starting riots, stealing and dealing like a rally
From New York to Cali
All over the United States
Hispanic, blacks, and white behind the jail gates

Hard As Ever
No fairy tale
People that portray to be stupid will fail
Hard times you got to be hard as ever

No back up or body guard
Sweat sizzling in the sun like lard
Dark skin was lynched
Fair skin snitched
We need to make a switch
Men bragging, their thangs are bigger
No black man wants to be called a nigger
It is like a weapon, Russian rootlet pulling the trigger
God has touched my spirit, I feel blessed
Family never guessed
That I would be in the music industry

Somehow the good Lord is a mystery
Seeing fools get peeled
Killed
Case shut, sealed
A minor
Old timer
Being behind bars for years
Not out with your peers
Went over the edge, drinking a 12 pack of beer
Dissected a man from his throat to his ear
A super fly, making girls hearts pound like a drum
Folks asking where you come from
Served time as an adult
Eight-grader, calling you dumb
Your mind went numb

Hard As Ever
No fairy tale
People that portray to be stupid will fail
Hard times you got to be hard as ever

This poem talks about someone trying to be hard and in charge. It also relates to trying to make it in the music industry and other issues to prove how hard one can be.

Action Comes First © 8/1993

Count to ten
Try to calm down again
Or lose my temper
No one to pamper
Dirty clothes left in the hamper
Trying to tamper
My food and drink at the skating rink
Clean the wax out your ear
So you can hear
What I have to say
You pissed me off anyway
Patience is a virtue
On probation with a ankle bracelet in at curfew
Playing me close
Let's make a toast
To all the player-haters, not a reason to boast
Critical thinking and using logic to the utmost
Betty-bye-bye
Ready to get 'high so high'
No sad story
Dismissed from the category
Dressed to kill
All up in my grill
Baby after baby
Need to get on birth control pills
Ruthless
Toothless
Careless
Bare this
Not scared one bit
Harsh words slip from my lips
Praying for a perfect fit

Action comes first
Life is a struggle, have I been cursed?
Action speaks
Talk is weak

No routine
Crisp and clean
No one was seen on the scene
Don't try to compare
Beware

Only find myself left in despair
End of my conclusion
There are different cases
Such as people in the mental institution
There is no real solution
That's what it seem
Can I wake up from this dream?
What a dreadful scheme
Did I really lose it this time, scream!
Using shaving cream
To shave off his hair
Head is left bare
Neva say double dare
My biggest concern counting all the money I earned
Thinking about how all that money was burned
In a state shock
I lost my man down the block
Shot
Trying to compete
Unable to stand on his own two feet
Dead body laying in the street
Money talks
Bull crap walks

Action comes first
Life is a struggle, have I been cursed?
Action speaks
Talk is weak

⁂

This poem refers to those angry with the world and only concern is money.
Biblically speaking, the Tenth Commandment refers to those that covet
their neighbor's wife, land, and things someone else has (neighbor)...found
in the book of Exodus. It can also be found in my spiritual inspirational
[Christian living] book called *The Day Begins with Christ*, which breaks
down each Commandment more in depth.

⁂

Ghetto Tactics © 9/1993

On the corner
Meeting up with some Fournier
Hustling to get the latest shoes on the market
To spark it
Looking at my troubles, singing the blues
No clues
Watching the death of my brother
Yelling and screaming came from my mother
Sons selling dope for money
Tired of the ghetto, living and looking bum-e
Whatever it takes to pay the rent
Ghetto tactic to the environment
Gambling busting raps
While playing craps
Popped aside the head, mom's snapped
Yo' homeboys laughed and clapped
From the scene
As if we were on a movie screen
Mom's smelled the weed
Bought and smoked earlier, taking out the seeds
To gather the amount we need
Light up the blunt
Broke walls in mom's house, some foolish stunt
Later was surrounded by cops, on top of a building
Hanging a nucca from the ceiling
Cops asked "Was it an accident or crime to a killing?"
Another nucca dead
From not selling the product and over words said

❊

This poem came to mind when I was seeing so much gangbanging and hearing about so many killings in the cities like Milwaukee, Wisconsin; San Bernardino, and Los Angeles including many urban communities.

❊❊

On the Hunt © 9/28/05

Hunters out on the hunt
Searching and killing anything in sight to get what they want
What is proper conduct?
When your gun is stuck?
Sell a product?
Back in the day, there was an old Southerner
Decided to run for Governor
Ghetto tactics, an old native
Now charged for illegal drugs in his possession, as the plaintiff
Only had a gram
Dead body found in his mansion near a Dam
Rammed
In a Suburban
Swerving
After smoking on some herb and
Turning the curve—in
A ditch
Son of a trick
When the cops pulled up, tried to cover up the evidence
No preference
Able to follow the tracks from my residence
Found myself in complete silence
Educator in the Suburban, left dense
Did it make a difference?
Who I was?
Words that flowed from my mouth, was 'all because'
I did not think I would be elected
Now my future career was wrecked
Another political man was selected

This speaks on a political leader that was crooked. His life and career choices reflect to the saying, 'any means necessary' by Malcolm X. Be careful with the choices you make since the Bible speaks on this: 'Reap what you sow'. In this poem, he reaped success at any cost and lost his position in office. Most likely, this political leader spent time behind bars for the rest of his dear life is what he sowed.

Got Tabs © 9/28/2005

First I checked the mileage on the car
Tires are full of tar
This is why I am stuck
Just my luck
Defuse to refuse
Looking for any information to incriminate
Willing to search for it at any rate annihilate
This fool put rat poisoning in my plate
Will this be the end of my fate?
Rejection dejection
Rather have an injection
Of cocaine
Shooting through my vein
At least I would be high to the utmost
However, it was not my choice
Lips are no longer moist
Fall back in my chair
Lights remain there
As I grasp on my last piece of air
Prefer to be on death row
Too much dado
Smoked up all the indigo
Got the tab
From an Arab
Grab the dab
Cutting his body into slabs
Gave his wife crabs
Tried to beat the heat
Is it a challenge? Who will I defeat?
Everything in progress, rumors drove me insane
All I could do was complain
Spies overheard the conversation, unable to contain
Information, now I lay here dying, unable to converse
Throat dry, sucking on my last saliva
Tapped my conversation at the Ramada
Corrupted in this universe
Wish I could put things in reverse
Feel like Cain walking out the Garden of Eden, cursed
Stash was wrapped in aluminum foil
Turmoil
Buried the cash deep, as my body turned back to soil
Money does not always bring happiness and joy
Flashbacks before the end: resurging being a little boy

Going out of my Head as I lay in my Bed © 9/28/2005

Jobs on freeze
Wife praying and crying on her knees
Moments later, cops bust in, "Seize"
My wife says, "Nucca please"
How could you put our lives in jeopardy?
Did you think, any?
What a catastrophe!
His excuse is that crimes have been going on for centuries
Barely can survive off these pennies
No child support from pops
Went behind bars that night with the cops
On welfare, WIC, food stamp card, hope it does not stop
GOD spells relief
With faith and belief
I can get pass this grief
Expect rappers to stop rapping
Is like stopping destruction from happening
Prisons full from pimp-slapping
187's flapping adapting
To the territory, who will be laughing
Once the guns are blasting
Later, got out of the game, changed dialect
To protect
Family from information televised
Dehumanized
To loving cash or addicted to the money flow
All my cards have fallen into the man of the law
Last call
Domino effect
Who will be next?
Game played me like Dofus
Acting ruthless
Only ended up broke, locked in the pen, toothless
Running the streets and from the FBI, in a hurry like Gingerbread man
'Catch me if you can'
Only for so long, I ran
Now I am locked behind bars, broken down walls, 'til I can't stand

This poem demonstrates how one man hustled for a buck to feed his family, covering up his devious schemes, and later serving a life-sentence for the crimes he committed. Same old story about many of our men and now even women are locked up behind bars for slinging a piece of crack-rock or illegal drugs to survive. Ask yourself: Is it worth the cost of your life being lost?

Quick Message © 9/1993

Youngsters out there
Beware
Don't play double dare
Stay aware
Of what sex is really all about
And drugs taking you out
Think it is cool to take a little ecstasy
To fulfill your fantasy
Watching your boys play with guns
Making runs
For your homey, selling, out on bail
From the county jail
Police have a warrant from a past drug bust
Running so fast, only leaving a trail of dust
Your homey took the rap for his old boy
Remember Satan comes to steal, kill, and destroy
Unable to avoid peer pressure
At 16, your old guy making you feel lesser
Than who you truly are
You can succeed and go so far
If you believe in yourself
Can't live your life for someone else
Keep your faith in God, everything will be alright
Pray in the morning, noon, and night
Don't give up without a fight
By doing what is right
The nonsense and killing needs to cease
Reminiscence on the happiness, good-times, and live in peace

Message Remains © 9/28/2005

Don't be a fool
Stay in school
Education is important
Instead of being someone's servant
Enslaved, so don't quit
Can't do anything without it
End up working for penny-asdic jobs
Or someone that kills, deals, and robs
To get the things they need
Lost in a life of greed
Never satisfied or enough
Even though times are rough
A message from a mulatto
Young sister named Deo
Name stands for godlike
Someone living a life for God, more Christ-like
Please be determined to make it
Shake it off, be able to take it
No matter what comes at you, never fake it
There is no need to smoke a joint
Brothers need an education to prove their point
I know there are some like Kanye West and Oprah Winfrey
that did not finish college
But it takes knowledge
Deeper than any power
Gleefully happy to see Jesus at that hour
On a quest
For a real success
Trying to find yourself, self-control
Allow God in your heart, mind, and soul
Always there when no one cares
Keep your eyes open and mind aware

I thought about all those that are illiterate, who skip school, and who felt that school is for dummies. For example, I graduated with honors. I had a chance of attending college after completing the eighth grade, which meant not ever going to high school according to my test scores and academic coursework. Yet, I chose to attend high school and college thereafter. Now, as I look back, I wish I had gone straight to college after finishing the eighth grade. Those that were enslaved fought to read and learn no matter what it took. Today, there is peer pressure, drugs, and other issues that will cause them to quit. Please don't give up and push. P.U.S.H. = Pray Until Something Happens. Also, please keep your eyes open, minds aware of your surroundings, and more importantly your ears open to hear God speak to you. You have a purpose and a calling, just open up to hear a Word from God. Amen.

Minding my Own Business © 9/1993

With only a few friends at the public park
Lights went on after dark
Heard a dog bark
It was no ordinary bark, it was time to leave
Laughed at a guy wearing a hair weave
Cops were holding someone
That was caught carrying a gun
We were just out to have some fun
Into this all broke out
Brother had no clout
Ran up to my homey
Acted like he did not even know me
Pulled out his gun slowly
My eyes popped out big
He claimed this was his new gig
A stick up kid
Was I going to live?
Thought deep inside, it was time to dig
My grave
Or I could have killed Dave
Flashbacks on taking Tai Kwan Do and other self defense classes
Watched my friends passes
To alarm me and prepare me
Moved so swiftly
Gracefully
Prayed Jesus would save me
But I heard a gun fire
Messed up my attire
Watched his body fall to the ground
Killer left unfound
Sirens, out of existence
Flashback of remembrance
God said, 'Repent and confess your sins', on my knees for repentance
Lord breathe into me once again
Played over and over again from Israel & New Breed
I realized from that point, God is all I need
Thank you Father for saving and sparing my life
I will never forget this night
Minding my own business
No witnesses
To see all the wickedness
But I was truly blessed
To live through this

Will U Rob Me? © 9/29/2005

On a high robbery chase
Pawn shops, grocery stores, banks, running like it was an Olympic race
Under God's grace
I held on my chest as I ran a rapid pace
Bumped into someone to rob
This man was someone who gave me the job
Working at MBNA, one of the biggest financial centers
I remembered his face as I enter
Noticed his Rolex and platinum watches
He noticed the tracks on my entire body
Holes in my clothes, sniffing at my nose
The dust before entering the party
Sounds of blasted music, drinking down some Bacardi
Making out with some hoes
Money goes Up this nose
A lifestyle he chose
Still alive
After the ambulance arrived
How did I survive?
Bullets flying from everywhere, grabbed a girl standing there
A new arrival
This was my way to survival
Her body was reliable
I had to duck
Blade in his hand, stuck
In her chest, crazy mutha-sucker
He stuck her
In the hospital, I was another number
Suddenly something covered my nose with some type of rubber
Suffocated
Hyperventilated
Rubber inflated
My nails clawed
Rubber had a flaw
Hole underneath, then ran from the law
Undercover cops were crooked yaw
Guess I got it all back
For robbing that old man Jack
As I broke free, I asked myself, 'Why did I do that?'
There was old man Jack
He paid them a stack
Gunned me down, down my body fell
Burning and yearning for life...breathe...breathe.... Gone, oh well

Gamble © 9/29/2005

Brothers getting sprayed
Bodies decayed
Do whatever it takes to get paid
Laid
In the dirt
An extrovert
That turned out to be a pervert
Desired women, many women, the younger the better
She fought, she kicked, I would not let her
Break free
Out on a killing spree
Only served a year in the penitentiary
One abduct
Struck
At any victim that pressed their luck
And tried to break away
Many women are glad that I am locked up, that day
Reminiscence on the gambling, clubs and casinos
In Las Vegas and Reno
Women were glamorous
Never suspicious
Grab them, seeing that I was delirious
Yea, they thought I was cute
Especially a man rolling with a lot of loot
Drinking down some Absolute
Stashed the blade in my cowboy boot
Flashing money while I was standing
Women appeared to be stranded
No ride, left abandoned
Caught up in a predicament
Once I offered a ride, felt I was heavenly sent
Did not know what that meant
Long as they got in my car, one tried to escape
Car crashing
Into a bus, people around asking
Why did I do it? Left confused
Too many women were abused
By my hands and manhood, bodies used
For my pleasures, strippers and prostitutes, what did I have to loose?
Then it was normal women, young girls, strung out on drugs and booze
Did not matter to me anymore, life or death, went berserk
Betrayed many women that I worked
So many lives were damaged and hurt
Raped and murdered any woman in a skirt

Time Ran Down © 9/1993

Why are people so furious?
Why are they so curious?
Taking things so serious
Acting delirious
Trying to make it off food stamps, assistance
Can you resist this?
Selling your stamps for cash
Dope man is on you're a**
Bills are getting too high
Barely can get by
Eviction note, evicted
Convicted
Caution yellow tape, place is restricted
Killings carried on in the home
Man lost his mind, killed family, and shot himself in the dome
Leave that crack alone
Another woman's husband stop paying child support
He tried to get full custody of the kids in court
Selling sports car as a sport
Making money under the table
But was unable
To pay something, so mom had to hook
Her body, then her husband took
The kids from her, saying she was unfit
Made her feel like the pits, this was not it
So she paid some guys to do him in, watched his neck get split
This is the outlook
Did she get hooked?
On the streets, on the johns, or cocaine
This bull crap damaged her membrane
Eating away at her brain cells
Gave up on God when everything failed
Now serving a life sentence in Wells
Where did the love fail?
Only can count the days spent in jail

Forced to Give up © 10/1/2005

Standing in the unemployment line
About to lose my mind
My house withered into pieces from the storm
Hurricane Katrina, trying to find a place to keep warm
Applying for welfare
People stop and stare
All on the news
You can say you feel sympathy, but I am the one singing the blues
What did you loose?
Constantly hear you complaining
But is your house remaining?
My man is no longer here
Police officers without a badge
Saying we on a shopping spree: jewelry and money stashed
We have no jobs or any cash
Mortgage companies want their money
What can I tell you honey?
My kids are going through puberty
There is no security
But as a parent, it is my duty
To feed my children, seeing that they are hungry
Use to be pudgy
What will I do?
Is there anyone out there for you?
There is Salvation Army and other agencies helping
Were you there when I was weeping?
Gas leaking
When I was on the streets
Praying for food to eat
Family members to take me in
How do I begin?

Screw You © 10/1/2005

I felt like I had no other choice
You no longer wanted to see my face or hear my voice
Forced to get a divorce
Endorsed
A blank check written out by you
Made me feel like some whore, it was just a screw
Now we are through
Awarded to the mental hospital for being distraught
I never can get that picture of seeing you get caught
This other woman in your arms
Must have put on your charms
Wined and dined her
Just like you did me, now it is only a blur
Are you with her?
Are you laughing at me now?
Once you seen my world go down
I thought you were my protector and my life
I meant every vow I said, when I became your wife
Later you treated me like a dog
Mind drifted away, calling me names like 'pig', 'hog'
Mind lost in the fog
This is my life on front page of the newspapers
Woman almost jumping from the skyscrapers
She got the vapors
The bad news and saw it with his secretary
He is already writing out my obituary
Love is nurturing
Not murdering
My inner soul, feels like an obsession or addiction
Can you feel my situation?
Breaking me down like a decimal
Broke me down on the mental
Just wanted him to be more sentimental
I was only ¼ of the fraction
No more addition, more like subtraction
Subtracting me from his life, his work, what a reaction!
Just came out of nowhere, went to the club for a little satisfaction
When we first met, he was so sweet
A man any women would like to meet
Even though I could stand on my own two feet
Let this man make me, break me, to feel complete
Now he is a pain in the neck
Watch who you select
To spend your life with, a life I need to correct

M.A.C.K. © 10/1993

There is a Mack in every situation
Do some investigation
This is not fiction or non-fiction
Mack will break you down and rub against you like friction
It can become an addiction
Watch how he/she rolls
Listen how the words flows
From their lips
Switching her hips
Wanting a weapon
If he is a ball-er, play-er, keep stepping
Guess whose creping
Cell phone turned off, hit up his pager, who doesn't have 'em
Dizziness creeping inside, then a feeling of hunger spasm
Hard to get pass 'em
Stomach started growling
People prowling
Hungry child hollering, borrowing
Money and begging for change from anyone
Judicial systems is where it begun
Money reads, 'In God we trust'
With God in our lives, we shall never go astray
Drinking down my money, cigarette butts in ashtray
Hard to make it another day
Changed my ways
Picking up bad habits
'Tricks are for kids, you silly rabbit'
But it also happens to adults, got to have it
Mack-money-making always checking clots
Hearing gun shots
While eating co-co dots
Female Mack's
No new jacks
To the rap game, no bull crap
To bust the move on the attack
By one snap
From the finger
Dead ringer
Rap artist and R&B singer
What a twist!
Imitators dismissed
Fellas getting pissed insist
That their pockets are bigger
No little wigger

Mack on © 10/1/2005

Music entering through my eardrum is pure funk
Bump it loud, sounds coming from the trunk
Bass shooting through your body
Rolling down the streets as if you are having a party
A thuggish, ruggish nucca not a punk
Hitting hard as a skunk
Throwing out the trash
Rolling in the cash
Mash dash the rest of the stash
Should I retire?
My life will expire
If I stay on, money roll is getting higher
They call me 'Sirer'
Homey's checking out the attire
Got this block on fire
Until I realized that I was wired
Need an alibi
Not much I can deny
Got me on tape, on cam
Now they know who I am
Not saying that I am all that
But I'll purr like a pussy-cat
Trying to keep my rep
Jealous hoes step
Post up
I am down to get up in that butt
To do dirt
Tag at it until it hurts
Putting my soldiers to work
A true Mack originated since birth
Not too many can compete on this earth
My word is born sworn
That I would get my mack on
Down with the program
Female Mack is what I am
Ask me do I give a hoot
Do you have the loot?
Oh shoot
Most men have to adjust
To the style I bust
Got a crush
Don't pressure me or rush
Or end up with no us

Peace of Mind © 1/1994

Two people meet for the first time
Love at first sight
Wanting and desiring you to be mine
Pouring a glass of wine
In the glasses, so many special nights
We shared
Got married young, not prepared
Times were spared
To show how much cared
Time passed, coming out of your mother's womb
Your youth went by so soon
Trapped inside a tomb
Of complete darkness
Miss how you use to spark this
In paradise, no motives to kill or steal
A passion, one would like to conceal
How they truly feel
No fortune, if I gamble, I want to win
Back at the joint again
Spend, spend, and spend
'Til you can no longer comprehend
Suspended in a time from way back when
Did not realize how serious things are, one blow to the face
Everything you've done was a waste
Felt like our relationship was running out of time
Can I keep up at this pace?
No one knows until you've had a taste
Feels like you are stuck, you cannot get out of
Looking and yearning for that love
Wanting to pick up the pieces and put them back together
Believing that my life will be better
Will I suffer forever?
A decade
Of this masquerade
Drifting away in our own escapade
My life is like walking through a maze
Mind floats away in the days
Hazed
Don't want to break down and cry
As time flies by
Wanted by the law
Cause a nucca broke your jaw
You pulled out a gun on him

You were the victim
However the jury
Caused you to doubt and worry
Will they lock you away and through away the key in a hurry?
A memory you cannot erase
The last look on his face
In complete shock
When I pulled the glock
Hoping no one would be suspicious down the block
Only way to survive
To stay alive
Does crime pay?
A parent tries to raise their child the right way
I wanted to live another day
Kids up for adoption, unable to accept
Time to redempt
Now I am held in contempt

Real Ma-coy © *1/1994*

Deo is coming to ya like this
Something you don't want to miss
On a conquest, I can't resist
The female with a big bra strap
Adapt To sister that can rap
Freestyle at the club, open mic
Giving the crowd what they like
Feel free to let yourself go
Get with the flow
Don't need clout
To turn this mutha out
On the dance floor is what I'm talking about
Don't press yo' luck
Especially when you are down to your last buck
Better strike it rich
Or you will get ditched
I cannot lie or even deny
That I am from the hood
No Mr. Roger's neighborhood
Color means nada to me
Get out of that fantasy
Despise
Your lies
Staring into your hazel-brown eyes
Only thoughts of getting between my thighs
Do you realize that you can't play me like a Barbie toy
You are dealing with the real ma-coy

Smoking a pack or 2 cigars a day
Hoping the stress will go away
Flashbacks, come back, remains in the memory
Remorse, only a source of recovery
Cannot think
Dang, I need another drink
Every time I blink
See a honey, 'pretty in pink'
As another brother dies, the second I wink
Things happen fools capping
Simply snapping
Over some bull
Bullet loaded, Trigger pull
Killed by instinct, anger
Friend, family, or complete stranger

Temper-tantrum, explosive... Look out, danger
Another brother dead
Sirens, lights, yellow, blue and red
Another brother bled
First murder was Cain
Killed his own brother, watch his mother's tears turn into rain
One blink
Did his killer even think?
Did his intentions or plans sink?
In his brain
Can you imagine his mother's pain?
Drank down some Southern Comfort to relax
Your income is not taxed
CD's waxed
Movies copied, trying to think things out rationally
Hit the sound waves internationally
Thug mentality into rap game mentality
Naturally
You got back to your old game
Even though you are big in the rap industry
Record sales made history
Killing this cop was on the air world-wide
I got to hit my weapon and trapped inside
From the cops, feds, and CIA
In my mind, that rookie had to pay
What the heck!
Had to keep that ho in check
My actions became suspicious
From my crew and media, think I went delirious
It was not appealing
The hustling and dealing
To be caught with the rookie's wife for some sexual healing
So I got that feeling for a killing
Dead from the real ma-coy
White rookie not treating me like no boy
Even though that trick gave me pleasure, pain and joy

Snap, Crackle, Pop © 10/2/2005

Snap, crackle, pop
187 on the rookie cop
Drop-top
Time stop ticking on the time-clock
Car was driving slow down the block
Guns shots blasted
2 minutes or less it lasted
Going at least 5 miles per hour
Blast you off, debris like the Sears Tower
After blowing up the spot
Ticker bomb dropped
Cops shopped around
Until the hit man was found
What's really going down?
Almost hit the guy with the 6-4
Police force could not tolerate this no more
Beating down the shooter in front of a candy store
African American and Hispanic kids watching
Closely watching how you are reacting
What really going on?
When the nucca is alone
Then his ho was stringing along
Thinking she was about to hit that ding-dong
But she realized he was thrown in the patrol car
She lost her superstar
Do I cry?
Realized I was pregnant with his child, why?
What I conceived, prepare to die
In the abortion clinic, feeling sorry for myself
I did this to no one else
But me

What U don't know (won't hurt) © 3/1994

Why did you slit
Your wrist for a hit
Arteries split
Blood spurt all over
Wishing your life was over
Wishing for a 4-clover
To win the jackpot
Your luck is hot
Until you indulged some Indio smoke
Cash all spent, left you broke
Choke until it ain't no joke
Choking on your own vomit
Once you became an addict
To heroine, cocaine, and ecstasy
Expecting this to bless thee
Cure from all your troubles and worries
Now you look and living dirty
Slipping stripping
Skipping meals
Body goes from being hot to cold chills
Nightmares
Demons stare
Where?
Right there!
Fire flares
A red demon standing there
Cold stares
In the face, looking in the mirror
Image of me standing there
Cold touches
Face flushes
Drug rushes
Through the veins from the crack pipe
How did I become hype!
All gone to the brain
Snorting up the lines of cocaine
On the small compact mirror, put in the cigar or compact
Almost had a heart attack by the hard impact

Where credit is due © 3/1994

Living in a world full of hate
Doing anything to get what they want, unable to wait
Killing, stealing and loitering, is it too late
To wake up from your mistakes
Complaining that you have no big breaks
Only out for what you can take
Concerned about the cash you make
Saying crazy stuff, until your blue in the face
Shut up when people put you in your place
What a disgrace!
Embarrassed to take 'em out
Trying to prove you got clout
Reputation is what you are all about
Cannot afford to put your rep on the line
What's mines is mines
Unable to appreciate the things you got
Putting yourself in the open to get shot
Willing to lay down your life on the hook
What a crook
Your life was took
Do not see your name in the good book
Shot
In the parking lot
Cops looking for ID
Never thought it would be me
So be grateful for what you have
Don't trip on materialistic things or when people laugh
'Cause you died on no one's behalf
God can take it
You can make it
Or break it
Break the habits and turn to the truth
Regroup
This fool could not handle being poor, seeking for success
But the game and the streets got the best of him, soul can rest
A man so hateful
Ungrateful
Talked a mouth full
Of bull
So conceited defeated
A lifestyle you cheated
But you could not cheat death
God's mercy and forgiveness, except you lost your breath
Now there is no hope of everlasting life left

Give me this and give me that © 3/9/2006

Give me this and give me that
When you make mistakes, sometimes you can not take it back
Just like the duo Kobe and Shaq
Give me this and give me that
Words can be full of bull crap
Especially when males think females can not rap
Snap back
This is the new era
From hip hop queens and divas: Mary J. Blige to Cierra
As they say, 'what is meant is meant'
Some believe female rappers on the low percent
However females like Salt N Pepa, Queen Latifah, and Missy Elliot made
it ancient
No longer need a man's consent
Give us credit
Once you hear it
Go get your concert ticket
Support us female rappers to the limit
Yo' girl, Deo is wicked
Wait until you hear her gospel tunes kick it
Through your speakers
Holy Spirit will make you get weaker
Hate when people spit and talking off the wall
This is to all of ya'll
Speaking negatively
Sorry this sister lives a life, spiritually
Whether I am living good
Or living in the hood
Whether females are cold
Young and old
Then you can see a sister coming bold
Reading from Proverbs and Psalm
To keep this home girl to remain calm
To gain wisdom and keep me under control
It should not matter on your sex, color or how old
To train your child up the way it should go
Do you feel my flow?
Pass me the mic
I'll give you something you like
Mixture of copasetic lyrics
Come on in
Flowing to the sounds of the wind
Fool you don't want none

As this blast through your eardrum
Don't ask yourself, how come?
Just be yourself
Quit trying to be like someone else
On a mission
Make your decision
I don't need a guy
To get by
Watch them blow by like another 'Ribbon in the Sky'

Roaring Rhythms © 3/1994

Flowing through the airwaves
From the Pacific Ocean to the mountain caves
Rocking and shaking up the graves
Mix up another jam
Faster than a money gram
Ask yourself who I am
Imitators scram
Give credit where it is due
Deserve props, instead tried to diss you
Another term for Buddhism
Is zen?
Where would we be then?
Leads to racism criticism
Do wa ditty
Hitting and crashing from city to city
Seeing children starving, no one to help
Cannot do it by myself
Should show your appreciation
To the Lord for every situation
Since he will bring you through, give him full dedication
Compassion for your neighbor and those that die
Funny how time flies by
Laughter and when you cry
Don't give up no matter how hard you try
God will send his angels to fly
To dry those eyes
Another saved soul, roaring rhythms in heaven sing
As the furnace dries
Soul will not rest in Hell
Amen for Jesus Christ, not a Lord of the Rings

Freestyling on the mic © 3/1994

Deo giving you a style I hope you like
Free-styling on the mic
Mc Lyte rapped about ruff-necks
God keeping our lives in check
One life to live don't wreck it
Respect it
Stay protected
AIDS is unselected
So many wanna B's
Fake O-G's
But I live my life like a sorority
Some artists get a lot of radio play
Seems like every day
Down with their own thang
Talking all that ying-yang
Looking for clout
No boy scout
Or sell out
A lifestyle we have to choose
Some will win, some will loose
Roxanne Shante was the first female rapper
Shortly after
Opened the doors
For many more to explore
Flowing hardcore
Females deserve their props
Does their status drop?
Cream of the crop
Striving to stay on top
From pop music to hip-hop
Willing to starve for bread crumbs
Dropping the bomb
Of my new lyrics, fighting non-stop
Got much flavor without letting the panties drop
Grew up on Slave, Rick James, Sly and the Family so funk-da-fied
Music artists tried
Sampling old jams to perform live
Sound still survived
Got others petrified
Stylistics, Isley Brothers, the classic
New groups get drastic
On plastic
Back in the days

Bands like Maze
Marvin Gaye with sex appeal and beautiful voice
Now Maxwell is the ladies choice
Down memory lane
Rain down your window pane
Sick of being alone
So the slow jams make me hang on
For true love in this new generation
For their new creation
Form of poetry
Autograph signing
Papers, contracts from the beginning
Old and new artists we love
Give thanks and credit to the Creator above

Too Smooth © 3/1994

Take a journey, then dive
I've been revived
Swirl like a tornado
To El Ferado
To spice up your taste buds
Tasty and chewy as milk duds
Back rubs
Making your bath water room temperature and hope in the tub
Turn me inside out
Without a doubt
My tiger, gentle and cuddly as a teddy bear
With that sexy long stare
The glare
In your eyes while sitting in Red Lobster
Later, hijacked by some mobsters
Appeared as an intelligent and generous guy
On the fly
My life was jeopardized to die
Last time to look at the heavens in the sky
The glitter and glow from the stars
Felt like light bugs in the jars
Captured, trapped under these circumstances
Taking risks and chances
After a few slow dances
Dressed
In black lace shift and Guess
Aggressed
My life was messed
Could I fight this battle?
In the bathroom with arsenic in my eye shadow
The doorbell rang
Then a big bang
Blasted down ten times, as I yell
Head started to swell
Dropped the aspirins down the sink
Could not blink
As I glide on the lipstick
Aroused by the noise, checked the place
Opened the door with a sex look on my face
"Hey baby, are you ready"
To go steady
He asked, "I'll ride in your caddy"
Calling you big daddy

If you have me
Will they fall for this, I was desperate
I will make out with them separate
No train
Just do it simple and plain
Gun held to my head
Will I end up dead
As I bleed
Where was I led
Stagnated in this bed
Rushed to expose
Clothes fully disposed
All I had to pose
Showing my figure, making me perform as I start to sing
Phone rings
Gives me the chance to break, escape
Had the whole incident on videotape
To prove to the cops of rape
Corrupt
To catch these rapists, murderers, lock up
I didn't want exposure or get noticed by a killer Otis
This fool is bogus
He started out as a gentleman that I went out to eat
Pulled out of my seat
He tried to make the night complete
However, he had secrets, skeletons in the closet
Lies running non-stop like a faucet
Toss it
Floss it
Almost lost it
Eating Chinese food
Back at his place to change the mood
Whole cha-bang
Then the bullets sang

Will it end © 4/1994

Continue to see people get shot
Always putting us on the spot
Jealous about the things we got
Are we just a spec
Thinking us have us in check
Watching stripes on those thrown in jail
Without bail
Raising hell
Nothing left to say
Because things don't go your way
May have some control
Wont let them take your mind and soul
A superstar
Riding in a decent car
Have a lot of cash
Cops on you so fast
Takes one guess
They're on you when you have success
Either blown to smithereens
Having babies in their teens
Killing is exposed constantly on the TV screen

Deep down inside © 4/1994

Sometimes I feel trapped in a gutter
Things in my mind start to flutter
In this world all alone
Living on my own
Nightmares, stalkers breathing on my telephone
Could it be an illusion
Draw to this conclusion
Use in
My intelligence, common sense
Repentance
From a life sentence
Change my life as the way it seems
To fulfill my dreams
Live today, dream of tomorrow
Happiness drifts away, feeling sorrow
What will be the outcome
To be a star forgotten where they came from
When will my fantasies come true
To pursue
Watch what I say and do
Because it can come back to haunt you
Out of the blue
Be prepared for all consequences
Wake up to your senses
Something to live for
Don't stop, go out and pray for more

Quit Denying © 3/12/2006

Quit denying
Fierce as a lion
Knowing that I am dying
Crying
Inside
No morals out with by pride
Persistent
For the dead presidents
Living in and out of your resident
People become distant
Singing in a chorus
Zodiac sign: Taurus
Memory of Delores
Much love to 3T, in remembrance of their mama
Though so much drama
Wild beat
Has been released
Don't expect a lot
Do not mean to put you on the spot
To prove that I am a real woman or not
Had a boyfriend smoking pot
Not perfect and choices we make
Can be a mistake
You give so much that only one can take
Everyone on this earth has a purpose
Life is precious, love hard to find on the surface
Others are in worse shape
No way to escape
Full of hate, anger, and fear
Asking ourselves why we are here
Quit denying
Fierce as a lion
Knowing that I am dying

On the Low Profile © 4/1994

Don't tell me to wait a while
With this vicious, cobra style
Slamming on top of the profile
Fortune 500 lays out all businesses
My concern is top 100 music list
Can I get any witness?
Sizzling hot
Putting fools on the spot
Because you got to give me all you got
Your cash
Only lasts for a short time, goes so fast
All on your mind is to 'sex me'
Test me
To see if you can get the best of me
Keeping your girl in line
With Deo on your mind
Woman all on your behind
Push it good
Break your back if you could
I know you like what you see
Taking me to ecstasy
Lusciously
Mysteriously
Looking sexy
Sweating me like honey
While I'm checking your pockets for money
Reverse psychology
A method of pimpology
All out to see what one can get
Do or satisfy the needs for one another to be set
Money, sex, car, doing things we will regret

Evolve © 3/12/2006

Evolution: the big bang
A world of apes did their thang
Apes later transformed into man
Cavemen were formed; do you believe this evolution stand?
According to Genesis 2:7, God formed man
From the dust of the ground
And breathe into his nostrils, winds from the Lord evolve around
The breath of life and man became a living being
God is the all-knowing, all-seeing

Evolve, Evolve
Will you allow your problems to revolve?
How will the evolution theory be solved?

The way, the truth, and the light shall set you free
Allow the Heavenly Father in thee
Seek His Holy Word
It is time to hear from the Lord
Control the tongue, else it can deliver blessings or curses
Start studying your Bible and memorizing verses
To allow it to deliver and restore your soul
Let the Holy Spirit unfold
Enter in your heart, mind, and soul

Evolve, evolve
Will you allow your problems to revolve?
How will the evolution theory be solved?

Not everyone is believing in that
Pain and pleasure with someone fat
Paranoia causing you to always watch your back
Handling all transactions with a gat
Walking the streets can be scary with trifling fools on the prowl
Biting other people's style
To make more money than a dump pile
Rising sizing up every John
Giving a large cut to Don Juan
To protect and attack your body like a vulture
Statistics claim it is based on the environment and culture
Persist to come at me constantly with all that bull
As Don Juan pockets are full
Buying me revealing clothes to make men drool
All along, I realized, Don Juan played me for a fool

Until I went to Sunday school
And realize that the world does not evolve around him
No longer a sexually abused victim
It was only a mind game with my body involved
Evolved
Around my own sexual weaknesses until the problem was solved

Evolve, evolve
Will you allow your problems to revolve?
How will the evolution theory be solved?

Finger at You © 4/1994

It is like a linear equation
Detecting the problem, solve it, until an invasion
Trembles while glaring at the picture, seeing a mirage
All weapons and plans are kept in the garage
Blood stains in the Chevy Dodge
Can you avoid the circumstance
As I glance in a trance
Until the case points its fingers at you
Now what is left for you to do
All the nuccas at the bar
Know who you are
Known as a huge superstar
Following you to the car
No longer living the same lifestyle you knew before
People opened the doors
But you still have your struggles in your life
Strife
To avoid the knife
In your chest
Pressure is great
Begging the murderer to wait
Something is wrong
For this to prolong
Black on black crime
What's wrong with our brothers mind
Need to help your kind
What are the consequences?
Kill of your race: Come to your senses
There are other outlets to overcome your expenses
Tricks will get tossed
Friend will be double crossed
To see whose boss
Turned inside out like Kriss Kross
It will just be your loss

Complete Silence © 3/30/2006

Some men are a sexist
Some cultural differences may cause them to be racist
Some wealthy man is driving a Lexus
One night, I pulled up in a local bar
In my Mercedes Benz car
To have a drink
Chewing on Double Mint gum so my breath would not stink
Watching the big screen TV
In the sports bar, wearing a leather dress and looking sexy
Kicking it with some O-G's
Old girlfriends
Want to kick it tomorrow, it depends
Reading all the eye signals, hard movements these men send
Able to apprehend
In my purse lies a 45-magnum
If someone gets dumb
Acting out like Madea, bodily injury can be the outcome
Buzzed and a little high
While walking to my ride
Opening my club soda
Who walks over
Body drops
Everything stops
In slow motion
No emotion
Heart stopped a beat
Fell down to my feet
Someone shot in cold-blood in the middle of the street
Head hit the concrete

Down to the Last Heartbeat © 4/1994

Stood still like a statue
With the gun pointed to my head, I was threw
No where to move or to run
Hands swayed with the gun
Calling me, 'Son'
Legs shaking, unable to hold my balance
Music faded
Body movements in a stance
He moved closer to my head
'Please Lord, don't leave me for dead'
Another aimed, beaming red
On my forehead
Ducked
Boy, did this night suck
Pulled my hair out as if it was plucked
Sirens roared, had to be the police
"Don't move, don't cease"
Surrounded the area, sweat poured like hot grease
Then I was able to run to my car and hold on my piece
The male I saw
Reported to the law
Witnesses at the scene of the crime
Good for that old swine
He had to serve time
That was a close call, either me or the man in blue
Whoa! I thought I was through
Down to the last heartbeat
Until the cops raided the entire street
Knocked the man with the gun to the concrete
Boy, do I want to hear
From an angel whispering in my ear
'You shall be saved'
You have been brave
Rescued from your grave
Now you bets to behave
Or spend time in Hell for eternity
No buddy, that will not be me
No more crazy stunts
No more women hunts
Sipping on warm milk
In my night garments made of silk
No more acting retarded
Right back where I started

Who dared?
To mess with the hearing impaired
That night I was totally scared
As the red flame flared
Guns blasted
Whole two-minutes it lasted
Blessed to remain on the face of the earth
God-fearing man now, able to move forth

Suspect © 2/1997

Unleash the wild beast
Last but not least
We cry out for peace
Shalom!
When will our men come home?
Reading another obituary
With revenge left in my memory
As I grieve at the cemetery
Listening to the commentary
Hair went bald
No applaud
No future career
Potential employers are not sincere
Check your friend's background
Observe their ways whenever they are around
No matter how cool they sound
This person you call your friend
Did you in
Incident could have been avoided, came to an end
Where have they been?
Spotted at the skating rink
Dressed in hot pink
Giving them time to think
Of a lie even though I knew they had a hard drink
Their breath lingered off a liquor stink
Need some space
Then get out of my place
This man had a good profession
Felt it was true love connection
Should have used protection?
Took full advantage of my body, in rage
Rape, due to the abuse, I pulled the 12-gage
How could I escape?
Closed all the drapes
Had to strategize a plan
Why I killed my man?
Had it recorded all on video tape
Naked in a black cape
Making a sex tape
Who could I manipulate?
No one, time to cooperate
To get a lesser sentence
Spoke to a priest for repentance
Never should have gotten involved

So What © 3/8/2008

So what, this problem was left unsolved
Too many involved
Secrets told
Another cock-a-roach
Took the sophisticated approach
Left me simply broke
Moved my monies to Swiss accounts
What a joke!
Thought he was for my best interest
Boy was I impressed
Dr. Jekyll, Mr. Hyde
Split personality inside
Noticed the hotel
Had a foul smell
Once was an admiral
Turned into a serial killer
Then a big time dealer
Transporting goods to other countries
Long time ago, collected pennies
Never had a clue
Allies and false identity too
Pointed his fingers at my head when we argued
Never imagined all that he did or what he is going through
Never got involved with him
Became one of his victims
Chances to find him were slim
So what if I ended up like this
Pleaded for my life, my last kiss
So what, even though he will be truly missed

Snappin © 4/1997

Yes, I am snapping
What is going to happen?
Thoughts are being unwrapped
Completely trapped
Thrown in a body bag, dumped in gutter
Mind started to wonder
His every thought is will I get caught
It was not my fault
People will know I came on my own will
Could this be surreal?
Does he do this to every female
He meets, keep his thoughts concealed
Body sealed
Then he meets another person
Money endorsing
Money wiped out of my bank accounts and what was in the will
Got my last dollar bill
Down to kill
Body lays still
Psychopathic
Money addict
Mental intellect is so pathetic
Notorious, obnoxious and devilish
Cut my body up like a relish
Premeditated murder and rape
Blew up my pearl tongue like a grape
Called this man
Ran as fast as I can
Slipped between his fingers
Man blasted me in two, dead ringer
He was so relaxed
Spoke in a structural syntax
No care for his fellowman
Broke my neck with the touch of his hand
Snapping
Capping
Slayed played laid
In the grave from someone snapping

Plans ruined © 4/1997

Plans to be architecture
Intrigued with his long lecture
Knew our lives were secure
But he quit school after the incident
All evidence lead to mental illness, begged for my consent
To be put in a mental ward
Oh Lord
We were in court again back on August 24th
Saw him in the back with some ugly whore
A date I could not ignore
I was pleading for his interest
Last score
Loneliness was deeper than before
That Tuesday
At 2:00 p.m. he let his plans get in his way
He refused to be admitted
I had him committed
At 8:15 a.m. had a job interview
But I had to confront you
Been six months since our last court date
Clean slate
New man in my life, worth the wait
Let him know that he still owed $238

Behind the Cracks © 6/1997

Behind the cracks
Kicking the facts
About fools that don't know how to act

Snorting and sniffing cocaine as if it is Afrin
Popping pills that ain't Buffrin
Pain ongoing, still suffering
From the side effects
Stop hanging with the rejects in the projects
He never protects when he erects
Shooting blanks
God is who I need to thank
Dead in the gutter
Blood spread like butter
Whole episode under cover
Dressing so gummy
Love slave
Until he walks to his grave
Misery loves company
Crack in two like Humpty
Left hungry and empty
No one shows pity
In the large city
Sit down to eat your meal
Homeless man nearby to steal
Find the season salt
You just bought
Was contaminated with arsenic
Poison in it
Due to sleeping with someone else
She was out for herself
It has no taste or smell
A headache was the symptom, not feeling well
Felt like your head would swell
Then cramps and dizziness
All based on jealousy and silliness
Leaving behind no witnesses
Dead as a door mat
To keep on sleeping with that dirty rat
And walk away with your insurance cash just like that

Whose the Blame © 6/1997

Why does one have to trip?
Once you make your grip
Cash flow, people trying to dip
Kiss on my lips
Later found in the garage
Started with a body massage
What you saw was a mirage
In some cases when a man becomes rich, woman yells "rape"
Incident with Tupac video tape
O-G's on lock down, getting high, loaded, and drinking a forty
His friend's jokes were corny
Talking about baby this and baby that because he is horny
One girl was caught in the circumstance
Fell for his lies and romance
Who takes that chance?
No time to think as you url in the sink
Guy you met in the club you gave me a wink
Staring at you in the hot pink
Now he's seeing a shrink
Manipulate as he starts to penetrate
Uterus clueless
To masturbation
To stir up the sexual sensation
Wanted a full demonstration
Speaking about your sexual fantasies confessions
Indulged with obsession
Mouth cut him like a sword
A man you could not afford
Drank some booze
Left when he snoozed
Heard a noise, electrical wire around his throat
The wire broke
Place lit up by the smoke
Had one option
To run to a new location
Watch him get his car, as he drove
Fire begun from the electrical stove
Got written a citation
From the police station
In court, he made a plead
For his misdeed
Received a misdemeanor for premeditated murder

The Point of No Return © 6/1997

Parents kicking you out of their home
Talking to you crazy and putting their lives on hold
Guess because they are getting old
Claiming I was out of line
For making a comment that was on my mind
Too old for a whipping or slapping
Mom, what is happening?
Tripping flipping slipping
Of the tongue, remember what you quoted
Cause I wrote it
I was praying for a fresh start
To say things from the heart
I do not want to fight
But unite
Had dirty pampers
In the hamper
For all the things I did as a kid
What I greatly forbid
Tell me not to do it, but you tried it
Don't hide it
Explain; don't play a role with your own child
At one point, one stage, you were wild
So, how do you expect to change my style?
Men disrespecting selecting
Where do most men fail?
Cannot work out their anger well
A heart my dad could not mend
From all the false hopes he send
Out on the prowl for awhile
The pleasure will cease
Pegging me for a piece
Of sexual passion at the least
Where have you been?
When I needed a friend
Not making a decent salary
Working at a factory
No capability of equality
With no sensuality
The point of no return
When it's my turn
You will learn
Some risks you take, you will get burned
Appreciate what you have earned

No Sympathy or Empathy © 7/1997

Very versatile
You cannot bite my style
I am adequate
You have to admit that you have been split
In half
Trying to follow my path
But you will be the last to laugh
As I sign an autograph
Yes, I am a star
Thought I would not get far
An array
As you're left astray
For someone that couldn't pay
Sipping on ooze
While on the cruise
Rapping is my tool
Someday Jesus' will rule
Reading the Bible is like being in school
Way down beneath
My soul will follow under a new leaf
Get your life on track
Once you die, you can never come back
What a lush!
Heroine to get a rush
You say, "Whatever"
Trying to be clever
This girl got a profession forever
Disinfect that bush
Wash your tush
Use Lysol or Pine-sol
Another anibosol
Another scheme to watch me on the TV screen
Dream
You could be me, a female with much detail
That rocks the microphone well
V. need to keep her hygiene clean
With Glycerin
Doing the hanky panky
Leaving the room all stanky
Out to gank me
Seen you down the hall
Making a phone call
Built like a potato

With a nappy Afro
Wearing two French braids
As I roll out of the room in my dark shades
Blew things out of smoke like throwing grenades
Intelligent diligent for the innocent
An experiment while I am on probation
Seeking for a spiritual revelation
At two o'clock
Seen you on foot down my block
Wearing one sock
Hit you in the jaw
Running away from the law
A female so raw
Had to put this chick in check
Total wreck
Paralyzed from her toes to her neck
Incarcerated
Blood pressure went upstate
Against this female I hate

No sympathy or empathy just one big catastrophe
Until you're hopeless and empty
With no sympathy or empathy

Maxing and Relaxing © 7/1997

Took one look
Was all it took?
To get me hooked
How I want to touch these
On a mission to please
Grab your car keys
Putting all assets on freeze
Arrive at the motel
Rock the bells
Not a single soul to tell
Hitting harder
Calling you my father
Big Daddy
Hydraulics got me bouncing in the 64-caddy
You're the adjective
I am on a sedative
Were both adults
It's no body's fault
That you unlocked the vault
Of pleasure and intimacy
You can have all of me
Sexually I desire thee
You can have any
Of this Good N Plenty
Simply you can have any part of me
Left me dry as the desert
As you insert
Much pleasure and pain makes it hurt
I cry desperately constantly satisfy
Love-making that you can beautify
A chemistry that neither can deny
Drowned in my tears, soak up on my love
Nothing else or no one I will put above
I will do everything
Just to make your body sing
Not another fling
Willing to do anything
From what my love will bring
A relationship so crucial
Feeling both mutual
Rejoice
When I see your face and hear your voice

Remain in the Game © 7/1997

What a She-Devil
Taking fools to my level
Such a rebel
Writing another manuscript
About tales of a crip
Counts against me, decriminalized
Legalized as your boys were circumcised
Cries lies no time to apologize, been cauterized
Judge or you shall be judged
Most of your homeys gunned down, did not budge
Still held anger in your soul from a grudge
Yelled in court, judge screamed "Contempt"
A night well spent
Jail gave you a free meal, education, and rent
Twenty sack
In your back pack
On H.S. grounds, money rolled up with a rubber band in stacks
Sucking on a tic-tac
Cops crashed
Money stashed
The cash thrown on the grass
Officer on patrol
Lost control
As they called for back-up, patty wagon
On the lock out for hustler known as the Red Dragon
On the corner, lighten up a cigarette
A girl you have not met yet
On the video set
See her all in the video
Hello it is time to lay low
Asking me if I would get with a smooth bro
Some gigolo
With top dough
Smiles and jokes
About the days when a nucca was broke

AWOL © 7/1997

The prettiest thing he has ever seen
Itching for nicotine
Chewing some Dentine
To freshen up his breath
Gave her the last piece he had left
Parents were devastated
With a man well hated
Just another girl he just met
Woke up in a cold sweat
Nightmare difficult to forget
Time to jet
In the next sequel
Met a man driving a Regal
He was my soul mate, my equal
Blown away by a gun
For something he has done
Basic instinct
Young black children dying like flies
Futures becoming extinct
Some at the precinct
Fingerprints and photos taken
Making one race look bad, no faking
More than what you thought
Once you were caught
AWOL
No one bails you out when you fall
Stall to make that one phone call
Homeys drop like dominoes
Over drugs and hoes
Bad foes
That has a flaw
With the law
Try to walk before you crawl
Rumble mumble stumble
Shed to pieces as the rock crumbles
Banished vanished
From society
Variety of crimes committed as a young-un
Ain't that something?
Dying over nothing
Screaming "Keep it coming"

About the Author

Adrienna was uplifted and inspired to write inspirational books, poetry and songs. Shortly later, God gave Adrienna other titles for upcoming spiritual books: *Day Begins with Christ; Unleashing the Spirit; Counsel Me Lord to be a Vehicle for Christ; Miss the Mark Series (inspirational/drama);* and *Desire at Will: Giving all the Glory to God through Prayer, Praise, and Worship -- Let it Overflow!*

She has written her first publications through Author House formerly known as 1st Books: *The Mystery Lies Within,* May 2004 and *From the Depths of My Soul: Collection of Poetry and Songs, Gospel/Religious Version,* September 2005

Adrienna has volunteered in youth ministries within the community (Big Brothers and Big Sisters Amachi program, mentor and tutor at Lad Lake Inc.) and church (youth leader and girls' basketball at New Testament Church, Milwaukee, WI). She also enjoys writing and reading in her spare time.

Adrienna has a Bachelor Degree in Information Resources/Technology and a Master Degree in Library of Information Science. She also participates in law training seminars through CLEO (Council for Legal Education Opportunity) and plans to pursue a law degree in the near future.

Printed in the United States
By Bookmasters